THE
UNBOUND
CLASSROOM

THE
UNBOUND
CLASSROOM

Chelsea Miro

CAST Professional Publishing
UNTIL LEARNING HAS NO LIMITS™

ISBN 978-1-930583-42-9 (paperback)
ISBN 978-1-930583-43-6 (ebook)

Library of Congress Control Number: 2019939676

All images courtesy of the author except where noted.
Cover photo: Witthaya Prasongsin/Getty Images

Published by:
CAST Professional Publishing
an imprint of CAST, Inc.
Wakefield, Massachusetts, USA

Bulk discounts available: For details, email publishing@cast.org or visit www.castpublishing.org.

This book is dedicated to all of the bright, complex young minds that inspire me to think about the ways you learn to understand yourselves and the world you live in. In particular, Lily, Lucien, Olivia, Matteo, Phoebe, Judah, Wren, and especially my very own little human, Soren. Watching your eyes open to the world and guiding your journey is my greatest joy.

Contents

Introduction ix

The Unbound Classroom Approach xv

Practical Aspects of the Unbound Classroom:
The UDL Connection. xviii

1 Establishing the Unbound Classroom 1

Road Map 2

Timeline 9

2 Finding the Lens of Your Unbound Unit 15

Two Approaches to Generating Topics 16

Generating a List of Lesson Topics 17

Generating a List Within an Established Curriculum 19

Next Steps. 20

Aligning to the Standards 23

3 Creating Lasting Knowledge Through Your
Unbound Unit 29

The Early Stages of Development 30

Beginning at the End 32

Defining Lasting Knowledge 33

Designing the Guiding Questions 36

4 Structuring Your Unbound Unit 41

Thinking About Your Unit 42

Developing the Culmination 44

Organizing the Scope and Sequence 50

Thoughtful Assessment 55

5 Unbound Is Variable: Developing a Unit
for Every Student 65

Three Ways to Think About Variation 66

Planning to Create Options in Instruction 67

Creating a Lead-In Project 70

Thinking Creatively About Integration 74

6 Fostering the Culture of an Unbound
Classroom 79

Building Your Community 80

Key One: Finding Comfort in Cross-Disciplinary Work . . 83

Key Two: Welcoming Diverse Learning 85

Key Three: Independence 87

Key Four: Support and Expectations 90

Final Thoughts 93

Appendix A   Designing With the UDL
Guidelines in Mind 97

Appendix B   Universal Design for
Learning Guidelines 105

Acknowledgments 107

About the Author 109

Introduction

I HAD NEVER THOUGHT ABOUT BEING A TEACHER BEFORE, IN LARGE PART BECAUSE I HADN'T REALLY EN-JOYED SCHOOL AS A KID. As a justice-minded, logical thinker, I often felt that school was unfair and didn't make sense. I couldn't figure out why I was learning what I was learning and what good it was to struggle through things that seemed irrelevant in the outside world. The idea of returning, of my own volition, to a classroom every day seemed wholly unappealing. In my junior year of college though, a friend convinced me to take a class called "The Craft of Teaching." She claimed the professor was "life changing" and that was enough to sell me. Brown University allows students to "shop classes" for 2 weeks and test out what they'd like to take, so I went into the first day intrigued but not sold. By the end of the semester, I was writing my essay for the Master's in Elementary Education program at Brown.

That class opened my eyes to the power of education as a tool for change. Education has the ability to empower students; I had never thought about it that way. A powerful education can open up a world of possibility to a young learner in any circumstance. I knew that education was important, but I didn't understand how the daily work of the classroom could build more confident and empathetic students by giving them the tools to understand and influence their world.

Take, for example, a quick lesson with a Langston Hughes poem: We could spend 30 minutes dissecting the meaning, interpreting each word, and rewriting it into digestible pieces, making students think that a poet's work is to confuse and confound language into unintelligible bits, needing translation to have any meaning. Or, we could put his poetry into the context of the Harlem Renaissance, allowing students to see how he takes the sonnet, a traditional English poetry form, and appropriates it to address the experience of the oppressed and to elevate the cultural capital of African Americans by mastering the form. In this class I learned that the purpose of education isn't to turn kids into right-answer seekers, bubble fillers, and fact-regurgitaters. The purpose is to open the world to their young, curious eyes and allow them the opportunity to explore.

To me, before college, education had been about managing and digesting content. Aside from a few classes, school rarely felt like it was about an open exploration of concepts relevant to the world today. This was particularly true in elementary school, where my strongest memory is the trauma of learning my math facts. As the last student to have my name written up on the wall for being able to do 100 multiplication facts in 5 minutes, my fourth-grade teacher would make the entire class stay in for recess and watch me take the test, then grade it in front of us all and comment at the end "well it looks like you'll all be in for recess again next week." I can still hear the chorus of groans from my classmates. I remember my dad sitting with me for hours, confused as to how I could never recall 7 × 8, no matter how many times we went over it. I remember thinking *I hate math. I am terrible at math. When I'm an adult, I'm never doing math again.* Despite getting quite a bit better at math over time, those feelings didn't dissipate until I found myself in graduate school, learning about how to teach math to elementary students. My professor explained how different brains process numbers in different ways. She said children shouldn't be forced to memorize, as that is not really what math is;

math is the logical pursuit of patterns, guided by critical reasoning. I hadn't seen a definition like that printed anywhere on the myriad of flashcards I'd drilled.

In college, I had studied American civilizations, a major completely devoid of disciplinary rules and regulations. I loved that aspect of my major and found it to be one of its most powerful features. Although some friends would say, "Oh, sociologists don't study that," or "Biologists are only interested in questions that can be proven," I had no limits on what was relevant and where my learning could go. Additionally, neither did my professors. My classes talked about mental illness, childhood trauma, survivor's guilt, racial oppression, women's roles in history, all in the context of America, but with few other bounds. As a result, we were able to have deep and fruitful discussions with thinkers from every discipline, integrating their thoughts into what I felt was a more robust, more complete view of the world of past and present.

When we'd discuss the societal aspects of mental illness, my best friend, who is now a psychiatrist, would talk about how medicine has evolved to see mental illness as a disease. Another friend, now an English professor, would talk about the way that literature changed views of mental illness by allowing people into the minds of those who struggle. I loved that my concentration taught me to think about all of these things together to create a wide and deep picture, rather than focusing too intensely on the role of just one piece. I would argue with my classmates about the limitations of thinking within the bounds of one discipline, telling them a whole world out there existed that they were ignoring in order to make their one-piece work.

College was the first time I felt that my education could align with my values and interests and most importantly, that I could follow my own curiosity. Of course, I had been interested in activities in school many times before, but that was merely by chance. The opportunities to pursue my own questions had been few and far between and were always limited by disciplinary restrictions. A paper for history had to focus on the impacts of something historical. A science project had to be about a scientific experiment and nothing else. When I got to college, we were able to shed those requirements and pursue questions no matter where they fell on the science or math, English, history wheel. In fact, any sense of these disparate disciplines was wholly abandoned, and the result was passionate, self-directed learning.

Then I left the comfort of undergraduate life and began graduate school, and immediately our classes were divided into teaching science, math, language arts, and social studies. I was bound again. It wasn't until a weekend trip home for my nephew's third birthday which helped me realize that there can be a world of elementary education without these restrictions. When I walked into my sister's house, I found Lucien, the just then 3-year-old, behind the DJ booth. He was changing records with ease, slowly moving the controls from one song to the next, matching the beats perfectly. He even scratched with perfect timing and rhythm. His skills at the turntable truly amazed me, not only because it was a sight previously unseen but because it seemed completely unthought of. DJing seemed like an adult, or at least, teenage pursuit. It wasn't, in my mind, a "kid" activity or interest. How many 3-year-olds even know what a DJ, or a record, is?

Back in school, I started to ask my other education-minded friends: What things are kids never even introduced to, let alone invited to try and learn? When they learn by doing something that interests them, what skills naturally come along with the process? As I started thinking about the skills students learn as they travel through the grades, I returned to the image of Lucien DJing his birthday party. The reality was that he'd learned many of the skills we teach toddlers. Being gentle is crucial to holding records and pulling records out of sleeves, and putting them back requires manual dexterity and hand-eye coordination, as does placing them and lowering and raising the needle. He had to understand the beat in order to move seamlessly from one song to the next. Even more impressive was that he was showing mastery of this range of skills even before he could read! Because he had to attach value to every record he looked at based only on the visual, he was able to recall what songs were on each one. A traditional preschool might have students holding baby dolls to learn what it means to be gentle; carefully coloring in the lines to practice holding pens; coordinating their hand to what they see, tapping on a tambourine to find the beat; and playing memory games with tiles to attach value to visuals. Although there's nothing wrong with these methods, I'm not sure that disparate activities aimed solely at teaching a specific skill would have spoken to Lucien in the same way as DJing, and aside from the baby, they don't have a lot of connection to the things he was seeing in his world at the time. Lucien was learning all of these skills in the practice of exploring, and his learning was grounded in a context, a context that made it relevant and interesting to him as a learner. The skills he was learning were necessary for him, which meant that building on them resulted in getting better at something he already loved. I realized that all of these are incredible tools in learning that are often neglected.

I started to play around with the idea that learning should be structured around a particular idea or topic, rather than restricted to a single discipline. I began to really think about the way we teach. We relegate the world into easily digestible subjects—math, language, history, science—but do students really learn best this way? And is this setup indicative of the world they live in or completely contrary to the way they'll be asked to think outside of school? Our focus in education has become so driven by content knowledge that we've neglected the type of critical thinking skills that would allow someone to see beyond the subjects.

When I started teaching in my own classroom, I asked myself: What if, instead of starting from the task (such as learning multiplication) and separating skills (multiplication tables) and content (multiplication word problems) into categories that don't exist outside of the classroom, we went the complete opposite direction? What if we took an idea or practice and then studied all the different aspects of it, allowing it to naturally guide our learning in a myriad of directions, all of which are authentic and engaged in this particular theme? I began calling this approach the "Unbound Classroom."

Of course, this approach is similar to what constructivist and progressive-minded educators have been advocating for years. It may also look a lot like project-based learning (PBL) at first glance. However, the Unbound Classroom approach differs in an important way. PBL tends to focus on answering a question or solving a problem. PBL takes a question or problem and asks you to explore a very specific aspect of it, coming to conclusions. I wanted to use a more general approach to relevant topics so my students would have more freedom to decide what problems or questions interest them within that lens—to take a topic and explore every aspect of it and from every possible angle.

The Unbound Classroom doesn't necessarily ask students to come to any conclusion. It asks them to broaden their understanding of a certain aspect of the world around them, to find its relevance and relationship to many different ways of thinking, numerical, linguistic, and so forth. Hundreds of questions are explored in an Unbound Classroom unit, sometimes simultaneously and often generated by the students themselves. Then, in the end, students are asked to share how the value of their newfound knowledge affects their understanding of the world around them. The Unbound Classroom asks students to be reflective, critical thinkers who engage in multifaceted contextual learning that helps them grow their skills and awareness while opening their minds to the intricacies of the world around them.

When I began unbinding my classroom from the strictures of discipline, I found the level of enthusiasm and intrigue drove my student's natural curiosity. My students were free to explore a topic they saw in the world around them, and the skills they needed to explore were relevant and necessary, rather than perfunctory and rote. They became engaged in learning fueled by their own curiosity, instead of top-down pressure from me or any teacher. I realized then that they were in the heart of an Unbound Classroom.

THE UNBOUND CLASSROOM APPROACH

Generally, teaching has focused on a distinct skill. There can be creativity in how to teach that skill—thinking about multiplication as repeated addition and having students count by a number to solve a multiplication problem is a great example of this. It's not drilling flashcards and making the facts rote, but it is still thinking about the skill in isolation and building the lesson around the specific skill. In the Unbound Classroom, a theme or topic comes first, and then skills are pulled out of it in the natural course of studying the topic, grounding the skills in a context. For example, if you were teaching through the lens of industrialism and the development of the auto industry, you could calculate how many windows were made every minute, 2 minutes, 3 minutes, and so forth in the early assembly lines.

Taking it a step further, you could look at the design of early assembly lines and figure out how and why they were structured that way. What made them far more efficient than previous modes of manufacturing? What could be done to make them more efficient? How quickly did they actually produce a car? How many elements did that require? Even more, a teacher might ask the students to look at the way engines are constructed and the types of questions engineers have to answer. What materials work best? How many times does a piston need to rotate to go a certain speed? How do you figure out how much gas you're burning? How much gas is required to produce cars, before they even begin consuming it? In this context, the focus is on building the skills of multiplicative reasoning, spatial awareness and design, business development, and decision making, but instead of building the lesson with the skill as the sole end goal, emphasis on inquiry becomes integral to a greater understanding of an interesting and engaging topic. Along the way, students are also learning other information and building additional skills: the introduction of automobiles to society and the changes that went along with that, car ads, how engines work, and so forth.

Take another example: When you're thinking about integrating math into your unit, you're not using a math problem and couching it in the language of cars (if four cars are built every hour, how many are built in 5 hours?), but actually studying cars and allowing the natural math required in that study to come to the forefront. Math is no longer isolated, irrelevant, and rote. Now, math is a dynamic, integral piece of understanding—something we see and use every day—and by understanding it further, we can answer questions and know more about topics that are relevant to our lives.

Kids want to know and understand how the world works. How many times has a young child asked you "but why?" They're naturally curious because there is always so much new, so much to discover. However, if school is always structured and presented in a way that highlights what they don't know and have yet to understand, they are going to spend their days feeling despondent and overwhelmed. If school is focused on building a context and helping students place knowledge and learning within that context, they will feel empowered by the pursuit of knowledge. They will not feel overwhelmed by what they don't know but instead will be motivated by their own curiosity. Do we need to think thematically rather than disciplinarily in order to do this? I think the answer is yes. Math, science, language, art, music—none of these subjects exist in the world in a vacuum, so why separate them only to have students enter the real world and then be expected to integrate them? By integrating disciplines early on whenever possible, wherever it happens naturally while studying a topic, we are bringing the real world into the classroom. This natural integration is one of the foundations of the Unbound Classroom.

With the Unbound Classroom, we are honoring the way that kids interact with their world today. I'm sure that, like me, you're constantly hearing things like "these kids now don't understand/can't do/won't do/are too attached to/only care about. . . ." These kinds of generational changes have always existed, and for a long time, teaching was the act of inundating students into a world of the past, the one their parents or caregivers grew up in. That has helped keep school feeling irrelevant—it has made school speak a language that feels old-fashioned and out of place.

Teachers now are looking for creative ways of engaging our students, so we want to speak to them in a language they understand. We understand that technology is creating a new type of student, and we're trying to figure out how to adequately adjust our classrooms to the language of the times. Kids are aware of the world around them without even having to leave their bedrooms. YouTube can take them anywhere, and apps can ask them anything. Kids are able to question what they see with increasing ease. Technology is changing the ways children view their role in the world and view their own agency. Kids don't need adults to answer factual questions anymore. They know how to take a phone and search "How long do whales live?" "How far away is the moon?" "Is there really a man on the moon?" They know how to find answers, and so the way that they understand the role of adults is changing as well. Children aren't looking to the adult next to them thinking—"Wow, that guy knows everything!" They are looking at their tablets with that awe. As the role of adults in the lives of children moves away from knowledge conveyor, it must move toward curiosity guide. Adults can help students spark more interesting, vivid questions. Instead of "How long do whales live?" a child can learn to ask, "What is the impact of climate change on the life span of whales?"

With the world opening up to kids, and kids being encouraged to forage and explore, the way we teach them needs to adjust as well. Today's child expects to be stimulated at every turn—entertained and conversed with. This means that their classroom needs to treat them as the different type of kid that they are. This is why I turned to the practices that led me to the Unbound Classroom. My role changed from "teacher" to "guide." I learned to see myself not as the bearer of knowledge but as the guide on a quest for understanding. When your students can find ways to answer the simple, the rote, for themselves, whether it's with a calculator or Google, it's time that we figure out how to help them ask the questions that are going to give them the most authentic, moving, and rich understanding of their interest. We need to give them the tools to follow their curiosity wherever it takes them and to see the world as a malleable place where they have an ability to make a mark. That is why we need the Unbound Classroom. We need a pedagogy that speaks to students in the language of the world they find themselves in—a world that is accessible, engaging, and complex.

PRACTICAL ASPECTS OF THE UNBOUND CLASSROOM: THE UDL CONNECTION

As I began to untangle the role of disciplines in my thinking and planning, I knew it was essential to ensure my lessons were reaching every student. Although I could think about creative ways to teach and think about a topic, I knew that if I didn't have a clear guide in my early practice that was helping me think about varying learning styles, students could be left out.

That's where Universal Design for Learning (UDL) comes in. UDL helps us think about the varying ways students learn, and addressing that in every lesson is absolutely essential to the Unbound Classroom. If the goal of the Unbound Classroom is to engage and empower learners to follow their own creativity, then it is vital that lessons are taught in ways that address the needs of all the students in the classroom.

When I first discovered the UDL Guidelines, I used them as a test for my units. Did my lessons take into account the many ways students take in information—that is, were they accessible in physical but also cognitive and cultural ways? Were the ways I expected students to tackle assignments or express themselves flexible enough? Would my lessons engage a wide variety of students with diverse levels of skill and preparation? Would students have enough support to persist and overcome learning challenges rather than getting frustrated and giving up. UDL is the perfect framework for creating an Unbound Classroom because it asks the practical questions that ensure you are reaching every learner in your classroom.

We've all likely sat in meetings or gone to conferences where educators have referenced "21st-century skills" and then gone on to share a few words like rigor and grit, as if making kids a little more able to handle challenge is going to change the world. The reality is that we need to look at the ways we teach, and evaluate what practices are and are not fruitful for our students. If you are in a school environment that affords teachers the freedom to determine how to structure lessons, you have a tremendous amount of pressure on you to develop lessons on your own.

On the other hand, those of us in schools with little freedom are under tremendous pressure to raise test scores, without having much agency over the ways we teach. As we search for more unique and relevant ways to teach, we are also faced with the added workload of creating lessons ourselves. That was where I found myself in my first classroom, and I found myself equally overwhelmed and enthralled by the idea of creating my own unit.

When I began planning my first unit, on the Chumash Native Americans, I realized that I needed some support. I wanted to make sure that I was creating an inclusive classroom environment that suited varying learning styles and abilities. Additionally, I needed to make sure that my unit was tied to learning goals that I could asses in some way at the end. It was this first goal that led me to UDL. Although I like to do a lot on my own, and I design each lesson, that is not to say that there aren't great resources out there that are invaluable in this process. The first of those is the UDL Guidelines.

In graduate school, we focused extensively on creating inclusive learning environments. We focused on varying learning styles, but also on welcoming the experience and life of each student into the classroom. It was broad and exciting, but also often very theoretical. As I set out to create my own units in my own classroom, I felt like I needed something very practical to ensure that I was developing a classroom where every student could learn. I had this discussion with a colleague as I was starting to develop my new and improved Chumash unit, and she asked if I'd ever heard of UDL. In time, what I found in UDL was a practical guide to inclusion—guidelines that made me think, with each lesson, about the different learning styles of my students and how to be sure to address them all simultaneously. The UDL Guidelines helped me take a daunting task—making sure my lessons worked for all of my students—and gave me questions to ask myself every time to think about the different components of each lesson.

The UDL Guidelines (Appendix B) are a foundational piece of each curriculum I create. I consistently return to them and ask myself, "Am I providing options for physical activity in this lesson?" "What auditory support is there for my students with visual processing disorders?" "How many options for expression do I have?" At first, this was a pretty rigid practice. I went through each guideline and thought about the ways that I could expand options for my students. Now, it comes as second nature.

In order to support your use of the UDL Guidelines as you read this book, in addition to references to the UDL Guidelines throughout, I have included a reference section at the end that goes through very practical ways to teach and address each guideline (Appendix A). These tips and ideas are ones I've used time and time again in my classroom to ensure that I am reaching students in a multitude of ways. As you begin on the process of unbinding your classroom, there are a few things that are absolutely paramount—using this process as a tool to engage *all* of your students is at the top. Above all, the reason I began creating units like this is because I felt like the way I was teaching wasn't doing everything it needed to do for my students; something was missing. The more units I've created, the more I've realized that by bringing the world into the classroom, the boundaries are taken off of learning. To that end, the physical, emotional, and mental boundaries of learning need to be mitigated as much as possible. Every student deserves an opportunity to learn in a way that excites them.

In the coming chapters, I will go through many examples of what the Unbound Classroom can look like, along the way giving you the skills and tools to bring this approach into your classroom. Teaching through a thematic lens and integrating the disciplines in the process can feel like a daunting task. This book is meant to guide you through the process of "unbinding" your classroom—moving away from subject-driven planning and toward a classroom that focuses on relevant themes, teaching the skills and content that go with that theme.

Although this book is geared toward K–12 teachers, I believe that this work is relevant and important for all K–12 educators. Many of my examples are focused on a classroom environment that has the ability to integrate the disciplines, because all the core disciplines are taught by the same person. This doesn't mean that, as a high school English teacher, you can't integrate other subjects into what you're teaching. A well-rounded understanding of Ray Bradbury's *Fahrenheit 451* can certainly include a history of book burning and censorship, but it can also get into some of the science of fire. What burns when you burn a book? What toxins are emitted into the air? What does it do to your body to inhale burned materials? How has fire been used as a symbol of destruction throughout history? All of these questions are interesting and relevant to the book without just focusing on Bradbury's dystopia. Maybe you'd look at that and feel it's a bit of a stretch—but that's the point. You are stretching the usual limitations and thinking about all the different ways to cover a topic. The additional benefits of integrating disciplines with older students are that they are even more able to participate in the process of generating these types of questions. Later chapters will discuss generating guiding questions, and for high school teachers, you may find that inviting your students into this process can be particularly fruitful.

Throughout the book, I will discuss ways that middle and high school teachers can adjust lessons and ideas to make them more relevant. If this work begins in elementary school, students will naturally continue to crave it in middle and high school. This need has been demonstrated in places like New York City, where schools like the iSchool teach through thematic modules that integrate all of the disciplines. Many of their students are coming from classrooms where thematic learning is a common practice.

What makes the Unbound Classroom unique in its approach is not only the combination of the thematic and cross-disciplinary, and the robust exploration of a topic, a move forward from project-based learning, but also its practicality. The goal of the book is to be a guide to take you through the steps and thought process of creating a unit that focuses on a theme and teaches all subjects and skills through that lens. After reading this book, you will have the tools to move your classroom away from an approach bound to discipline-skill goals and toward a classroom where the learning process is naturally grounded in a context.

In an ideal world, you'll have some time, summer or a break maybe, to go through and map out a full unit, but if you don't that doesn't mean that you won't find relevant pieces in here. Each chapter is structured to guide you through a longer process of creating a unit, but also includes smaller lessons and activities that you could try tomorrow to get a sense of what this work looks like in your classroom. The book begins by taking you on a tour of a thematic unit in my classroom—studying the Chumash Native American tribe. From there, we'll look at how UDL and approaches that focus on how to reach every student naturally integrate with a thematic, integrated way of teaching. We will go through how to choose a topic, developing guiding questions and lasting understandings, structuring your unit, reaching all students, and implementing the unit, all while exploring units

I've developed. Through this approach, you will see not only the value of this way of teaching, but also the outcomes: engaged, excited students, who are capable of harnessing their curiosity to drive their exploration of topics relevant to the world around them.

Welcome to the Unbound Classroom.

1

Establishing the Unbound Classroom

> GUIDING QUESTION: *How can you take one topic and stretch it across the disciplines?*

THE GOAL OF UNBINDING YOUR CLASSROOM IS TO ESTABLISH A CONTEXTUAL FRAMEWORK FOR YOUR STUDENTS' LEARNING, ONE WHICH BRINGS RELEVANCE, INTEREST, AND CURIOSITY TO STUDENT'S LEARNING. As teachers, we need all of these things when we learn too. As we begin this process of creating cross-disciplinary units, we will ground your learning in a context and framework that makes this work feel attainable and realistic.

This chapter will lay the foundation for your learning. We will go through the frameworks used to create thematic units and dig into the practical reasons that makes this work incredibly relevant to today's learners. We will set goals for your learning, and for your students, and make the sequence and time line for this process clear. This chapter will be your road map to the Unbound Classroom.

ROAD MAP

To guide us along the process of creating thematic units, I will walk through the chapters using a unit I created on the Chumash Native Americans as our foundation. As you hear about the ways that each chapter will structure your learning and process, the unit will help you envision what this work will look like in your classroom. There are beautiful moments to be had in any classroom, those times when a student comes to your desk and says "I get it now!" Or you hear something so insightful during a turn-and-talk that you have to take a minute to commit it to memory. These moments allow us, as teachers, to feel capable and confident in what we're doing, because we see our students becoming capable and confident.

When I began teaching third grade in my first classroom, I was handed some threadbare pieces of the last teacher's curriculum just a few days before the school year began. Toward the back were two packets and some handouts on the Chumash Native American tribe. A traditional third-grade topic, the study of local tribes often relies on field trips to local museums or historical centers, some worksheets, and maybe an art project. It tends to be dry, and moreover, inaccurate. For example, the teacher before me had the students make tepees as part of their study. Tepees are more suited to nomadic tribes as they are easily assembled and disassembled, but many people erroneously believe these are the sole home structure of all of America's native people, and maybe that's because it is what they had learned in third grade. The Chumash of the Central Coast of California lived in stationary communities in small dome-shaped homes made of a dried local reed, called an ap. When I learned that the students last year had made tepees after a week of filling in notes from a packet, I was not only frustrated by what had been taught before, but I was overwhelmed by the realization that I was going to have to create an entirely new unit from scratch. I had asked for curriculum materials all summer, and when the administration finally gave me the materials, it was just a few days before students were to arrive, and while I could push the unit back in the year, it still felt daunting to create a unit about something I didn't know in just a few months.

The Chumash unit wasn't a topic I got to pick myself, but it was something I knew I had to teach because third grade traditionally covers the local Native American tribe. I also knew there were high expectations from parents and students for what this unit would entail because it had become one of the "rights of passage" of third grade to create the Chumash tepee village. Never mind the glaring historical inaccuracy—parents wanted to see that village and students wanted to make it. How would I integrate my own way of teaching with something so firmly established? (In Chapter 2, we will explore these conundrums while also taking a close look at what it will look like to develop a topic entirely on your own. When you develop a topic, you'll begin to see all of the ancillary skills and ways of thinking that you can pull into this unit.) With this Chumash unit, instead of seeing my job as a deliverer of facts, I began to think of myself as a ship's captain, guiding my students on an adventure where they would pick up information and experience that was interesting and relevant to them. As you read this book, I hope you, too, will begin to see yourself as the guide to your student's learning, as opposed to the conveyor of facts and figures.

Once I committed to creating a new plan entirely from scratch, I had to think about what I wanted my students to learn. "The Chumash did not live in tepees" is certainly something I wanted my students to walk away knowing, but I wanted to think about what understandings would be valuable for them to have beyond this unit. Basically, I wanted them to know why this unit was relevant to them and what they could expect to get out of it. This brought me back to another framework I've used in the past when developing units that I find particularly relevant to thematic units: backward planning with enduring understandings and essential questions—inspired by *Understanding by Design* by Grant Wiggins (we'll go into the Unbound Classroom version of this process in Chapter 3). By planning backward, you always know where you want students to end up. Lasting knowledge and guiding questions carry the work that gets you to the final culmination.

For my Chumash unit I wanted my students to have the lasting knowledge that:

- *The Chumash were a rich and vibrant culture that used the world around them to drive innovation and progress.*

- *The way the Chumash lived proves that the environment around us provides much of what humans need to survive and thrive.*

The questions that I wanted to drive my students learning were:

- How have the ways we interact with the environment around us changed?

- How has the ecology of California's Central Coast changed since the Chumash?

- What did the world of the Chumash Native Americans look like? Sound like? Smell like? Taste like?

- How can we bring the world of the Chumash alive for the rest of the school to experience?

The lasting understandings helped me focus lessons on a goal that was broad enough that I could get every student there, while also specific enough to be of true, lasting value for my students. The questions helped guide the different aspects of their learning and also encouraged me to think about different ways to integrate disciplines through this study. We ranged from scientific to sociological, and each question can be approached in a myriad of ways. With these tools in hand, I was ready to begin framing my unit.

With the Chumash unit, I wanted the unit to end with the students forming an interactive Chumash Museum. Although this created an experiential learning opportunity for the rest of the school community (a little like the tepee village), the main reason I wanted to do this was because it turned the students into the teachers. It asked them to decide what was most relevant to young learners about the Chumash and to explore what most resonated with them. They could understand why we studied so many different aspects of the Chumash way of life and put all of that information together in order to make a vibrant picture of the lives and culture of a group of people from the past. Next year, in fourth grade, the students would study the Chumash after contact with the Europeans. I wanted to make sure that my students understood that the world of the Chumash was lively and accomplished. With this interactive museum, the students owned their knowledge. Even more than deciding what was relevant, they had to think creatively and critically about their newfound knowledge by deciding how to best share it. The museum gave them something to work toward beyond just knowing a list of facts about the tribe.

The students were invited into the world of the Chumash and then were asked to think critically about their way of living. When students began making tea that could cure headaches, and putting diatomaceous earth on their skin as sunblock, they were able to understand the importance of the natural world to the Chumash. When they started exchanging shells as currency, they understood that trading goods has transmitted culture and information across groups of people for thousands of years, and that the value of money is what it's worth to someone else. As they thought about the challenge of building canoes out of driftwood that traveled hundreds of miles to the Central Coast, their assumptions of Europeans as the first to travel the seas were challenged, and their knowledge of the sea as a bearer of a multitude of valuable things was expanded. The students' natural inclination to ask "why?" was not only welcomed into the classroom during this study, but the students discovered they had the tools to find answers themselves.

The museum project required that whatever the students decided to study, whatever they found most fascinating, they had to ask themselves why anyone should care about this. And they had to be ready to answer the question. They were not just asked to bring the world of the Chumash to life; they were also challenged to understand why this mattered to life today. This is the essence of making any subject, especially social studies, relevant; I wanted my students to walk away feeling that learning about the Chumash was important and valuable and even more, that it was exciting to teach others about some of the facets of traditional Chumash life. In Chapter 4, we'll start by discussing how you'll create a culmination, like the interactive Chumash Museum, that is engaging and exciting for your students. We'll also look at creating a scope and sequence and how to create thoughtful assessments that help you authentically see what your students have learned. Once you've decided on a culmination, you'll develop lessons that will help students successfully synthesize their knowledge at the end.

Once the backbone of your unit is in place, you'll be ready to develop each lesson. As soon as I knew where students needed to be in order to create the Chumash Museum, I decided to take them on various tours of the Chumash world. First, we needed to know what it looked like. When you're studying something historical, it's important to give it a visual space in a student's mind. Kids love to imagine! We talked about the different aspects of the village, the homes (aps), the chief's house, the central fire, the location along riverbeds with specific types of reeds, all of these integral aspects to Chumash life.

Then each student designed their own village within a set amount of space. They had to calculate the circumference of various-sized aps along the way, and they had to measure everything included and have dimensions on their drawing. This gave them a place to imagine the world of the Chumash. A student with an extensive Individualized Educational Plan (IEP), who was often pulled out of the classroom and had been labeled a "discipline" problem, created a 3D scale model of a village, with aps he made out of clay to fit the exact dimensions he calculated. The smile on his face when the museum opened and guests oohing and ahhing his model brought his past and current teachers to tears.

Additionally, throughout the 6 weeks of this unit, the kids kept their own daily journal where they were asked to imagine

FIGURE 1.1. Students learn to make a traditional Chumash drink, starting with crushing acorns.

their lives as a Chumash person. They could pick their age, gender, and standing within the tribe. Each day they had to include at least one piece of information they learned about the Chumash into their journal. If we'd just made a traditional drink from mashed acorns, students would describe drinking or making that as their character (Figure 1.1).

Just like math isn't the memorization of rote facts, history isn't either. All of these aspects allowed our Chumash study to become far more than a social studies unit. Teaching any topic well requires a dynamic approach, looking at the theme in as many different ways as possible. After we built our content knowledge about the Chumash through multidisciplinary activities, we moved to the higher-level thinking tasks: What can kids do with their newfound knowledge? I explained the many different ways that you can look at times in history, studying money, people, medicine, plants, etc., and students were able to choose the way they wanted to continue to study and joined others interested in the same topic. This was their time to explore.

We started with each group deciding on a more specific topic to cover in greater depth. For example, after learning that the Chumash had their own currency, the economists decided they wanted to know more about what that currency looked like and how it was used. *Did it work with other tribes? How did they acquire currency?* The anthropologists wanted to learn more about the purpose of traditional dance. *Was it connected to religion? Was it for fun? Exercise? Who made the dances? Who taught them?* From here, students used their newfound research skills to go through the resources in the classroom to find answers to their self-generated questions. (Creating engaging and exciting lessons that build the knowledge and skills students need both in their life and time in school in order to have a thorough and deep understanding of any topic is the focus of Chapter 5.)

After several field trips to museums, and Skype calls with two people who had founded and directed museums, the kids were ready to further challenge their understandings of the Chumash by developing ways to teach others and present their new knowledge in a museum. This culmination truly assessed their ability to synthesize knowledge in a way that a test never could. In this unit, there was a lot of group work toward the second half, as the students divided themselves up based on the way they wanted to continue to study the Chumash. There were anthropologists studying dance and games, and another group studying religion, as well as groups of economists, ethnobotanists, and linguists. Each group came up with a way to share its information in an interactive exhibit. Each booth had to have graphic representation of the new knowledge, an activity, and a handout to give guests at the end. The booth, handout, and activity needed to be historically accurate, and they had to be able to show where they got their information. The resulting museum was nothing short of incredible.

In a large field next to school, guests were greeted by student docents who guided them through each of the museum's programs. The ethnobotanists showed guests how to make traditional acorn mash and had a natural apothecary. You could ask them about an ailment, and they would show you the plants the Chumash would use. Sunscreen? Here's some diatomaceous earth—the white powder will reflect the sun without absorbing into your skin. Stomachache? Don't worry, the ethnobotanists would teach you how to brew traditional Yerba Buena tea! The students' pride as they shared their knowledge was obvious. Most importantly, this format allowed each student multiple ways to access the material and engage with it. *Every* student participated. *Every* student learned.

There is a lot of community work that needs to happen to make your students confident enough to embark on their own, self-directed learning process. (In Chapter 6, we will talk about what a classroom community needs in order to be ready for these types of units.) At the same time, it takes time as a teacher to grow accustomed to life in the Unbound Classroom. Your students will need you a little bit less, and you'll find yourself a lot more curious about what they are learning and thinking. This chapter will help you create an unbound mind-set—how to think as a teacher who is free to explore an interesting topic alongside the students. You will all be explorers together, and even though you'll be leading the expedition, the voices, skills, values, and needs of each member will be integral to the process.

TIMELINE

This book is a tool for you to use as you see fit. You may read the whole thing, or you may find that there are three or four pieces that really resonate with you and are attainable in your classroom. One of the keys to great teaching is flexibility. What works for one student may not work for another. In the same way, what you get out of this book might be totally different from what another teacher pulls out. I have tried to create a wide variety of resources for you to take away. There are connections to standards, tips on using the Universal Design for Learning (UDL) Guidelines, and lesson ideas that could all be used in your classroom tomorrow. On the other hand, if you do decide to create a full cross-disciplinary unit, be sure to give yourself the time and space to ruminate. As you decide on a theme and begin your research, see what information feels most pertinent to you. Explore how learning about this topic feels—it will help you empathize with your students as they learn. The more you can all be in the mind-set of a learner, the better.

Once you have a topic and some of your research is done, assume it will take you a few weeks, at the least, to get the unit mapped out with essential questions and enduring understandings, as well as a scope and sequence. From there, it just depends on how long it takes you to craft each lesson. This work could be done in an uninterrupted summer week, month, or over the course of the school year, little by little. The Chumash unit was created little by little over the course of the school year (and once the unit got started, if I'm being perfectly honest). The jazz unit you'll read about next was a winter break project. The journalism unit you'll see in Chapters 4 and 5, along with the eminent person unit toward the end, was created over summer break. And the natural disasters unit was quickly crafted over spring break. For many, the topic and some of the enduring understandings were fashioned long before I was able to actually sit down and map out the lessons.

Deciding on a topic can take weeks, or, if you don't have any choice, it can take no time at all. The enduring understandings and the lesson framework will take time to play with, but if you have a strong sense of what you want to do, I suggest getting this down and then giving yourself the most time to actually create the lessons. Once you get started teaching your unit, give yourself time and space for reflection on each lesson. This will help you improve the unit the next time you teach it, and you can tweak any upcoming lessons as needed. Remember that you are not racing toward a test in 3 weeks where every student needs to understand how to do long division or they'll fail. Your goal is to broaden your students' understandings of a particular topic, while building developmentally appropriate tools and skills. This work takes time, and when you find that a lesson doesn't do its job, don't just move on to the next. If that skill, tool, or knowledge is valuable enough to be a lesson, then it is valuable enough to be revisited.

WHERE YOU ARE NOW:

We've talked about how I came to create my Unbound Classroom, where it fits into current pedagogy, and why I think it's valuable. We went on a tour of my first unbound unit, giving you a road map of the process to come. Now you're ready to get started building your own unit!

This chapter is really meant to be a tour through an unbound unit. An unbound unit takes a topic and explores it from as many angles as possible, stretching students' knowledge and asking them to engage in the topic in multiple ways. You can take an existing unit and revamp it into a cross-disciplinary marvel!

KEY POINTS TO THINK ABOUT AS YOU GO FORWARD:

- Think of your curriculum as a living document—it is always subject to change and adjustment. Give yourself time to reflect on lessons when you can, and make a few changes each time you teach it. This is not just to ensure that it's as impactful as possible but also to keep it interesting for you.

- Remember that relevance is important, and anything can be made relevant if you approach it the right way. The way you position your unit is going to be the way your students understand it—if you're excited about teaching it and the material is engaging to you, it's much more likely it will be for your students as well.

- As a teacher, this process may feel foreign to you. Remember that feeling—that is how your students feel frequently when they are asked to learn new things. When you get frustrated and want to stop working on it, take note of that, and try to think about where that may happen to your students. Empathy is a crucial tool.

- The Unbound Classroom is an invitation to welcome your own creativity into the classroom. I'm not talking about borders and fonts, but your own curiosity, your own learning process. Respect yourself as a vital member of the classroom. It's your learning process that will guide your students. The better you understand the ways you learn and approach new topics, the better job you can do thinking about the ways your students will understand learning in a new way.

- Be patient with yourself.

2

Finding the Lens of Your Unbound Unit

> GUIDING QUESTION: *What topics are relevant and exciting to you, your students, and your community?*

MAYBE YOU'VE JUST FINISHED THE SCHOOL YEAR, HAD A GOOD VACATION, AND ARE READY TO START PLANNING FOR NEXT YEAR. Or maybe it's winter break and you're finally getting around to revamping that fractions unit everyone struggles through. This chapter is going to help you find a topic and begin structuring a cross-disciplinary unit. Ideally, this step begins when you have some time to really think about what your students need and what topics will feel relevant and engaging to them, while also highlighting skills you know they need to gain this year. Do you have time over the summer to dive into a new approach to curriculum creation? Are you in need of a respite from the more structured work of your classroom and ready to test the waters of interdisciplinary work? The great part is that these units can be made as long or as short as you want (you're making them, after all!) and can be used to suit the needs of your classroom, whatever those needs may be.

This first step, finding a topic, may not feel relevant to you if you're a high school history teacher, with every topic already laid out, but you may find that this chapter helps elucidate new ways you can approach topics you've taught before. If you're in a very structured environment where you don't have the freedom to teach whatever topic you choose, for example, somewhere with an entirely scripted curriculum, you will find guidance as to how you can begin to think about restructuring your approach to be more inclusive of multiple disciplines. Ideally, you've got time to work through the creation of the full unit, but even if you don't, you'll find that selecting topics you'd like to explore and possibly guide students through learning is an inspiring start to the process of unbinding your classroom.

The first step to creating a cross-disciplinary unit is to select a central theme. When picking a topic, there are some important aspects to take into consideration:

- What your interests are

- What the students' interests are

- Where the students are developmentally

- What fits with your established curriculum

- What your resources will allow

An important aspect of picking a topic, especially if you have the freedom to choose a topic you want, is that you can draw from your own experiences and expertise outside of the classroom. Bringing in your own interests allows your natural learning process to kick in and can help you identify misconceptions and roadblocks early on.

TWO APPROACHES TO GENERATING TOPICS

In this chapter, we'll look at two different methods for generating your list of possible topics. The first is entirely self-generated. This is great when you have freedom in your classroom and can dive into any subject as long as you're able to meet the standards. The second involves going through your established curriculum and finding areas where you can take a single-subject unit, like one focused on fractions or early American colonies, and transform it into a multifaceted cross-disciplinary unit. After deciding on a topic, you will take further steps to align the unit to the Common Core Standards (or any other standards your school may use). Next, you'll go through your lessons and see where you can build points of connection between disciplines.

GENERATING A LIST OF LESSON TOPICS

Let's start with ways to generate a list when you have total freedom to design a unit of your own. This initial phase is really just brainstorming; taking notes and keeping track of your ideas will make it much easier to eventually pare down. Start by looking around at your interests: What kinds of books are you reading in your spare time? What are you watching? What are some subjects you'd like to learn more about but haven't had the time? If you're connected to the subject matter, with a genuine interest in what you're exploring, the process of deciding on your topic will be a lot more natural and exciting for you. It also gives you an opportunity to genuinely model this process for your students, showing them that adults pursue new interests too.

A few years ago, I started watching a Ken Burns documentary on jazz. It got me thinking about how jazz music has so many important aspects to it that it could be a great lens through which to teach multiple subjects. Although I didn't know much about the topic, other than that I enjoyed listening to jazz, I thought this could be a really interesting route to take. Not only did the music form develop during the early 1900s when African Americans were using the arts to influence American culture, but it represented a freeing of music itself. Additionally, the mathematical component of jazz really intrigued me. I kept thinking about how these incredible artists developed such strong senses of timing, which, when you look at it simply, is an impressive ability to rapidly manipulate values in your head. Although you can absolutely be a musician and not have a sense of numbers, music is easily mathematized, and that's just what I needed to be able to fully integrate this unit across all disciplines. I thought back to multiplication as repeated addition, and then realized that bars of music are easily counted using repeated addition, skip counting, and multiplying (all the same thing under different names). Then beats can be seen as dividing the bar, or fractional pieces of the bar. Just like in math, music is based on repetition of patterns. Learning how to read and manipulate those patterns is a fundamental skill that exists in both. Although K–6 teachers can begin to make these connections with simple skills like reading measures and beats, a high school ecology course could mathematize the repetition in bird calls and compare it to the patterns in human music. A geography teacher can search Google to find the article "Surface Topology in Bach's Canons" by Tony Phillips and then connect mathematical models for topology to the high and low pitches of their favorite songs. The possibilities for connection are endless once you start breaking free of the mind-set that math looks like equations on a page and nothing more.

In this initial step, you want to be looking for topics that are relevant and interesting to you, like jazz was to me, but also for ideas that will spark the interest of your students. A great way to find these subjects is to engage with the culture of the student body. Take a walk around the neighborhood: What does it look like? What questions does it make you ask? There are so many things happening around us that we rarely dive into in the classroom. Take time to think about how the architecture around you developed. What is the history of your school's area? What languages do you see written or hear spoken around you? Is there any form of public art (whether sanctioned or not)? If you're in a rural environment—what's grown around the area? How was that decided? How was the land broken up? It is worthwhile to take the time to dive into the community your students see every day. A cross-disciplinary unit is an opportunity to open the eyes of your students to something they might not otherwise get in school, but that doesn't mean it needs to be something far from their world. It is also an opportunity to show them that the world they live in is worth learning about. Particularly for students in underserved locations, the world they read about in books and the things referenced in math word problems (i.e., Joan made 10 *croissants* last week . . .) rarely show the world they see around them as a valuable place filled with opportunities to learn and grow. Your unbound unit is a powerful chance to show students that the classroom is an extension of their world, not a glass box meant to keep them separate and "safe" from the challenges that lay outside.

GENERATING A LIST WITHIN AN ESTABLISHED CURRICULUM

Generating a list of possible topics when you have an established curriculum is a bit more technical. I suggest using your curriculum map to review the topics you cover and highlighting those that stand out to you as meeting one or all of these criteria: needs to be revised; needs to be redesigned with every learner in mind; has multiple, clear connections to other disciplines.

As you begin looking at your established units, ask yourself: Has this unit been successful at meeting its goals in the past? Do I still enjoy teaching this unit? How does it look in light of the UDL Guidelines? Does the unit have clear potential to be expanded across subjects?

At first, you'll probably find that your social studies topics seem the most applicable to that third category. Certainly, social studies is a great place to start, both with UDL Guidelines and with creating a richer cross-disciplinary unit, since it tends to be a subject with fewer established curriculums than, say, math or science. I would challenge you, however, to also look outside of social studies, even if it's just for the purpose of generating your list. Math can be a great place to enliven and connect units. For example, take a simple geometry unit on area and perimeter. These two topics present huge possibilities for connection—a unit on architecture or engineering would tie in perfectly here. You may find you've got a great idea for a unit about local or national landmarks, like the Statue of Liberty, which culminates with kids using their knowledge of area and perimeter to design their own landmark. If they've learned scale and proportion, they can create scaled models, all of this while writing about the building, either from the perspective of someone designing it or simply in order to describe it and work on detailed, descriptive writing.

In another direction you might ask your students to design their dream homes, think about the area and perimeter of each space, and then write about great architects like Frank Lloyd Wright and Antonio Gaudí. There are so many directions in which this simple math topic can go. As soon as you start thinking about the ways these topics are used by adults, studying art and architecture, for example—think about the way an engineer might look at a Gaudí building. How do you create such crazy shapes with the building materials and technology they had at the time? What materials were used? How have building materials changed over time, and why? Why does architecture change over time? Is it always a result of function? Or does design also have its own value? These are all questions that an adult studying this topic might want to explore. As you start to think about each unit as if it were a hobby you had decided to dive into, you'll find an endless possible number of ways to connect to your math curriculum.

NEXT STEPS

After you've created a list of topics you're interested in, there are several steps to take it through in order to narrow down to the final choice: First, you'll build your own background knowledge and possibly assess the background knowledge of your students, then you'll look for developmentally appropriate resources on the topic. These steps will help you shorten your list, and then, once you start thinking about how to connect out from that theme, it will begin to become clearer which theme is right for your students right now. Ideally, this work will be done before you start the school year or during a break when you're ready to dive into creating a new unit. That said, if you have the time, you can really create a new unit at any point in the year. At the very least, you can start brainstorming topics for the next school year at any time. You can take the process of unit building slowly and especially the step of homing in on a topic. At some point, it may just come to you—we need to study jazz next year!

Once you have a strong list that has at least a few topics you're excited about, it's time to narrow it down. Begin thinking about the ways you can develop this curriculum and connect it through the disciplines. Start by going through your list and crossing out topics that you're sure you aren't interested in or may not be right for your students. Then, try to narrow down your list to three or four topics you're interested in exploring.

Now it's time to begin building your own background knowledge. If you're already fairly familiar with some of the topics, you may not need to do as much research. Start with a simple Internet search and see what information you find. With jazz, after the documentary, I started with a few biographies online of famous musicians I was already familiar with. Treat this endeavor like the research phase of a paper. Right now you just want to learn as much about this topic as you can in an amount of time that feels comfortable. As you learn, take note of how much information is appropriate to your students' level. With jazz, there is obviously a tremendous amount of information that is not appropriate for third graders. I looked at how much of it could be avoided without presenting an altered or inaccurate picture and felt that there was still plenty of material to cover while still speaking honestly about the development of jazz and the lives of musicians.

As you research, start thinking about how your topic connects to other disciplines. With jazz, I started to learn about some of the great musicians' songwriting techniques. I thought about one of my favorite artists, Nina Simone, and her protest songs like "Why? (The King of Love Is Dead)" written in response to the death of Martin Luther King Jr. and thought of a writing activity where students pick a current event and then write lyrics in response to it. They wouldn't compose the music, but they would write in free verse and have to come up with a repeated chorus.

Before you go further, you need to check out what resources already exist on this topic for your students' age group. If your school has a library, that's a perfect place to start. A quick Amazon search will help you see what books are available. It is helpful for a unit to have some anchoring texts that you can use to further explore the topic. It is not necessary—I didn't have one for the Chumash unit—but it certainly makes things easier and will help broaden your focus and bring in ideas and people you may not have thought about. Additionally, read-alouds are vitally important for young learners, so linking a text to the unit allows for a crucial point of engagement for your students. For K–6, I like to have at least five or six high-quality picture books, and for Grades 3–6, at least one chapter book that can be an in-class read-aloud, or guided reading book. For middle and high school, a great independent reading book that suits the theme can help bring homework, and traditional writing and reading activities, into the context you are building. For my jazz unit, I was lucky to find a myriad of options for picture books, but the chapter book took a bit more digging.

Lastly, you may find this is a perfect time to test out a brief lesson on one of the topics you're interested in to assess student background knowledge and interest. For example, you could use one of the picture books you've found for a read-aloud one day in class (assuming you are in session while working on developing a new unit). This is an easy way to introduce some topics about jazz and see if your students are interested and what they already know. Additionally, in Chapter 6 you'll read about lead-in projects, which will help you introduce the topic and assess student background knowledge once you've decided on a topic and built your unit.

In this initial phase you don't need to flesh out each lesson; you are just looking to see if there's enough to work with so that you can connect the unit to all of the disciplines. Later on, we'll figure out how to see beyond each discipline and create lessons that don't just connect the topic to each subject but ask students to integrate them.

ALIGNING TO THE STANDARDS

Once you've narrowed down to one or two topics, you need to check that you can align enough activities to the standards. This step is meant to help you choose between these final two topics and plot where your lessons need to go and what skills students need to cover. Going through the standards now both ensures that you'll be able to meet them and gets you started thinking about what understandings and skills this unit can cover.

The standards often feel like a burden when planning. Change that mind-set, if you can, when you go to plan this, and see the standards as a tool. Below you'll see the ways that I've individualized and processed the standards for myself. I used Common Core, but this work is relevant for any standards you may need to use. Look at them and think creatively about the ways you can achieve this work in the classroom.

Like everything, you will find that some standards are more of a reach, and others fit perfectly. As I go through the standards, I am constantly thinking: *How can I fit this skill into my unit?* Below, you'll find some examples of how I've thought about integrating the standards with the topic.

STANDARD	CONNECTION/ POSSIBLE LESSON(S)
CCSS.ELA-LITERACY.RL.3.4 *Determine the meaning of words and phrases as they are used in a text, distinguishing literal from non-literal language.*	Shared reading with a jazz song where we talk about literal and nonliteral language. Music is a perfect place to explore this standard in depth.
CCSS.ELA-LITERACY.RI.3.3 *Describe the relationship between a series of historical events, scientific ideas or concepts, or steps in technical procedures in a text, using language that pertains to time, sequence, and cause/effect.*	Reading biographies is a great way to engage with informational text and do lessons on cause and effect. Creating a timeline of jazz music by reading through multiple informational texts. For K–4 learners, timelines are a great way to encourage temporal and sequencing language.
CCSS.MATH. CONTENT.3.OA.A.1 *Interpret products of whole numbers, e.g., interpret 5 × 7 as the total number of objects in 5 groups of 7 objects each. For example, describe a context in which a total number of objects can be expressed as 5 × 7.*	This standard lends itself perfectly to counting in time with music. We can figure out the "counts" and how many there are. For example, the teacher can say "how long would an eight count for five" take. Students would think about counting to eight five times, a total of 40 seconds. This is also a great standard to explore through poetry and music. For example, create a poem that has five lines per verse, each line is six words, a total of three verses.

In most any school, you're asked to address the standards in one way or another. For me, this often felt like a burden when I was starting out developing my own units. It also made it much more appealing to rely on established curriculums with the big "Meets Common Core Standards!" seal of approval on the front. When I began creating cross-disciplinary units though, I found that the standards were actually a fantastic tool to challenge myself to think about the ways that I can ensure I'm thinking about the skills my students need to have. Just like I did when I looked at what Lucien was getting out of DJing, I always want to be sure that I am thinking about skill building while designing a unit. Looking at the standards allows me to see the natural skills that are inherent to a thorough study of our topic through a developmentally appropriate lens. Just like the UDL Guidelines, the standards can serve as a valuable check to ensure your unit is covering the skills your students are expected to have.

It is important to note, however, that the standards are incredibly discipline-oriented, even subdiscipline-oriented, so integrating them will pull you out of thinking *across disciplines*. I suggest starting with an activity that explicitly works on the standard and challenge yourself, as you begin developing the lesson, to see ways to integrate other disciplines. That said, every lesson you teach in these units will not span every subject, but the idea is that the unit as a whole integrates all subjects and has sufficient opportunities to blend and blur the lines.

For middle and high school teachers, the standards in your own discipline are a useful tool for similar reasons as above, but more valuable will be looking at the standards in other disciplines. Whether or not you try to fully address them, it will give you a sense of the topics and tools students are expected to have in their other classes. Knowing this information will help you branch out in your unit and address topics that are relevant to their other classes, even if other teachers aren't interested in integrating the unit with you.

WHERE YOU ARE NOW:

Keep in mind when you're deciding on a topic that building a thematic unit is an incredible opportunity. Look at the world around you. Look at your students and see where you can meet the needs of both. If your students are feeling disengaged, if school isn't speaking to them, find out what does, and create a unit as a tool to bridge that gap. Even if it's a unit on video games, pop music, or *Diary of a Wimpy Kid*, or one that just carefully includes topics that students are interested in, help your students see themselves as capable agents in the world around them. Let them follow their own curiosity, and give them the agency to be truly active members of their classroom and their learning.

CHOOSING A SELF-GENERATED TOPIC:

- Think about what is relevant to the community and interesting for you and your students.

- Make a giant list—you'll have time to pare it back.

CHOOSING A TOPIC FROM AN ESTABLISHED CURRICULUM:

- Look beyond social studies and try to connect other disciplines, like math, to its real-world uses.

NEXT STEPS:

- Build your background knowledge.

- Narrow down to a few topics.

- Gather relevant resources.

- Use chapter and picture books for younger learners.

- Create a quick and easy test lesson.

ALIGNING TO THE STANDARDS:

- Be creative.

- Use the standards as a tool to think about developmentally important skills that are found naturally in your theme.

Creating Lasting Knowledge Through Your Unbound Unit

3

GUIDING QUESTION: *What do I want my students to get out of this study?*

THIS CHAPTER WILL FOCUS ON DEVELOPING AND FRAMING YOUR GOALS FOR YOUR UNBOUND UNIT. By starting with your end goals, the lasting knowledge you want students to carry with them after the unit, we will have a framework to support lesson design. Each lesson and activity will tie into these end goals in some way, allowing you to align lessons with a set of fundamental principles that you want your students to learn, and guiding questions that you want them to continually use to guide their inquiry. An Unbound Classroom is still subject to goals; you always want to have the end in mind before you begin. By first thinking about what students will get out of this unit, it makes it easier to structure each lesson by thinking: How will I get them to these lasting understandings? What skills need to be built, what tools need to be explored, what knowledge needs to be engaged and strengthened, in order to have students understand some of the fundamentally important things about immigration, public art, jazz music, etc.? This thinking will guide you through the next step of designing an unbound unit.

THE EARLY STAGES OF DEVELOPMENT

The first time I developed an unbound unit, sorting out the lasting knowledge and guiding questions was the most challenging part. I was teaching fifth grade in Rhode Island as part of my graduate school training. In addition to student teaching and classes, we were required to observe as many classrooms as possible and reflect on the varying styles we encountered. I had been visiting schools all around the country doing these observations, and I found, time and time again, that I was most impressed and most fascinated by my time in classrooms that were integrating subjects into thematic studies. After seeing a particularly amazing culmination at the Greene Hills School in Brooklyn, New York, where kids learned about the East River and the Hudson River, and created two rivaling interactive installations about the history of each river, I realized the power of cross-disciplinary units. Students were proudly discussing the changes in the types of fish as a result of human actions and how those impacted the ecosystem in the river. They were seamlessly integrating science and history. In fact, they weren't even aware of the differences in these disciplines because the two topics had never been presented as disparate.

I decided after this trip that it was time to start crafting a cross-disciplinary unit for my classroom. I began by thinking about what topics I felt my students needed to have more information about and thought I would develop a unit on the Middle East. A few days later, a massive earthquake hit Japan, and I was struck by the questions my students asked me—"Can an earthquake like that happen here? What is a tsunami? Can a wave wash over the whole country? Can we predict when natural disasters like these will happen?" Then with all of the aftereffects, like the breakdown of the nuclear plant, the questions moved to the human impact and the ways that we do and don't prepare for these types of disasters. My students brought my first cross-disciplinary unit topic to me, because their natural curiosity went in so many directions. Although I knew then the topic would be natural disasters, I had to think carefully about what it was specifically that I wanted my students to learn from this study. I knew I didn't want it to be purely the science of natural disasters, but instead be more focused on the varying ways that humans react to and prepare for them (Figures 3.1 and 3.2). I wanted to use natural disasters as a lens to examine global differences. In order to do this well, I knew I had to first define what exact pieces of information I wanted my students to leave this study understanding, and what questions would help me frame my teaching in order to get them to the lasting knowledge.

FIGURE 3.1. Stations about different natural disasters allowed students to become "storm chasers" and move around the room gathering background knowledge as our first lesson of the unit.

FIGURE 3.2. A station about volcanoes.

BEGINNING AT THE END

Planning backward is one of the best ways to build a strong, scaffolded (where support is carefully planned so that students have a lot of assistance at the beginning and as they build tools and skills, they are able to be more independent) unit that focuses on creating lasting knowledge about big ideas. It is divided into three stages: First, identify the outcomes and results, which is done by developing strong, relevant, durable understandings and vital questions that set a template for how to get students to naturally find the lasting knowledge. The second stage focuses on ensuring evidence of understanding by creating thoughtful assessment tools. The final stage is articulating the actual scope and sequence of the unit—the lessons you construct to support students' developing knowledge and guide them to the lasting knowledge. We will focus most of our time in this chapter on how to identify the heart of your cross-disciplinary unit, what you want your students to know when they're done. Throughout this chapter, you'll be asked to think: *What is the purpose of my unit?*

DEFINING LASTING KNOWLEDGE

The backward design process begins by identifying what you want students to learn. There will inevitably be a huge amount of information that falls into this category. This is really all the pieces you want them to get out of this unit, not just the big picture but little tools and skills. Thinking through all of these pieces will help you down the road when you're mapping out your lessons, but right now, it's most valuable for deciding what big ideas you want your students to understand at the end of the unit.

There are three rungs each piece of information should fit into:

1. What is important for students to be familiar with?

   • Think about this outer layer as: What do you want your kids to hear, read, view, research, or otherwise encounter?

2. What is the prerequisite knowledge students need to have in order to learn what they need to learn in this unit?

   • The middle layer is comprised of important knowledge and skills that kids will need to know to complete the activities of the unit.

3. What are the big ideas and important understandings that we want students to take away from this unit?

   • Lastly, the big ideas are the most central: What do you want kids to remember after they've forgotten the details?

FIGURE 3.3. A student compares the effects of earthquakes in Haiti and Japan.

I had only one intended learning outcome for the natural disasters unit (it was a rather short unit because I had only 3 weeks to fit it in): *As a result of human interaction, natural disasters affect different areas in varying ways.* With this learning goal, I structured the unit around the idea that human action has a huge role in the effect of a natural disaster on a community. This focus pushed my unit to cover far more than the science of natural disasters and opened my students' eyes to the multiple ways that natural disasters affect people, based on more than just geography (Figure 3.3). A huge number of different, smaller tasks and skills are required to get students to this final understanding, but in crafting it, my hope was that the next time students saw a hurricane or earthquake on the news, they thought about how it would affect the community, what resources would be available, and why.

In fact, I recently heard from one of the students in that fifth-grade class. She is now a 12th grader, and when Hurricane Irma hit Puerto Rico in 2017, she and her classmates immediately thought back to that unit and raced to put together a drive for supplies, anticipating that Puerto Rico may not receive the same resources to support the community as Florida and Texas. These are the kinds of outcomes you hope to have. If nothing else, these students remembered that the same natural disaster can strike two places the same way but affect them in vastly different ways depending on a number of variables.

It's important when thinking about lasting comprehension that you limit your unit to two or three lasting pieces of knowledge at most, because you want to keep the unit following a clear trajectory. These are really meant to be big ideas that the students walk away from the unit knowing. In writing these pieces of information, you are directly addressing the content knowledge you want students to take away, while also ensuring the unit is valuable and relevant to the world they see around them. Lasting knowledge can also specifically target students' common misconceptions or misunderstandings. For example, a unit on Islam could have an intended learning outcome that helps students separate what they hear on the news about fundamentalists from the types of Islam practiced by the vast majority of Muslims around the world.

Additionally, lasting understandings are a crucial aspect of developing a cross-disciplinary unit because you can focus on a variety of knowledge that all links to the same topic. For example, a unit for young learners (K–2) on lions could have three learning goals, each of which relates the topic to a different discipline.

- *Lions are an essential apex predator, crucial to their ecosystem.*

- *Illegal poaching and deforestation are rapidly changing lion's habitats.*

- *Lions have had important roles in traditional myths and folktales throughout history.*

Each of these understandings allows the students to think about different aspect of lions and approach this study in a way that engages multiple disciplines and encourages them to make connections across the disciplines. They will begin to see how lions' role in the environment as an apex predator plays out in the myths they read, where lions symbolize strength and courage. By putting together their knowledge throughout the unit, the students will begin to see and understand the role lions have played in history both out in the wild and in human history. Additionally, they'll see the changes in humans' views toward these animals, and the earth, over time. Where lions were once revered subjects of myth and folktales, they are now trophies to be hunted, a way to symbolize man's dominance over even the strongest of creatures. A study of just the science or just the myths would miss all of these critical pieces that can be deduced by a cross-disciplinary unit that addresses the myriad of ways that lions can be studied. The learning goals are the guiding force helping you weave together the disciplines in order to create lasting knowledge that is relevant and interesting in multiple ways.

Overall, lasting knowledge goals:

- Are relevant outside of the classroom.

- Make it clear why the topic is worth studying.

- Elucidate the larger purpose for smaller activities and skills.

- Focus on large concepts, values, or processes.

- Are understandings that can be applied to other topics and situations.

DESIGNING THE GUIDING QUESTIONS

Guiding questions help drive the planning process by giving you a consistent inquiry to return to and explore. If lasting understandings are the heart of the unit, then guiding questions are the veins that guide the exploration. They can be overarching, covering a big idea, or topical one. They are more specific to details of what your lessons will look like than the enduring knowledge. You want to create guiding questions that address both the big ideas (the lasting understandings) and the content knowledge that students will need to have in order to reach the learning goals. Thus, some may be giant questions with complex answers that will be pieced together through the unit, while others may be more straightforward and address smaller topics that are necessary for students to understand. Back to our example about lions, an overarching essential question may be: *What is the role of an apex predator in an ecosystem, and what happens without them?* Whereas a topical question might be: *What cultural role has poaching played in sub-Saharan Africa?* The first gets to a big idea that the lion unit is helping students see, while the second focuses on a specific aspect of the unit that will be important for students to understand in order to get a wide picture of the topic.

As you build your guiding questions, try to think of at least one overarching question for each piece of lasting knowledge you've decided on. The understanding doesn't need to answer the question. In fact, you don't want your guiding questions to be clearly and concisely answerable. The process of answering them should be the work of all of the lessons of the unit. The question should guide you toward the understanding. Under each leading question, you can then think of more topical ones.

In my natural disasters unit, my questions were:

- How do regional and global politics affect the impact of natural disasters?

- In what ways do human-made environmental changes alter the impact of a natural disaster?

Although both target the human role, the second also requires an understanding of what causes a natural disaster, and what its effects are, as well as the positive and negative ways that humans deal with the unpredictability of the natural world.

Here's another example and one that may speak more to those teaching in the upper grades. For a unit on Islam with an enduring understanding directly addressing misconceptions relating to fundamentalism, an essential question could be: What is the history of religious fundamentalism? This giant, overarching question isn't one that you would expect to really cover in full, but your topical subquestions will guide its direction and help you begin to think about what the lessons need to focus on. Your topical questions might be: What is the history of the concept of jihad? What caused the modern wave of fundamentalism in Islam? What is the mainstream Muslim view of terror groups like ISIS? What does fundamentalism look like in other religions? As you look at these subtopics, the focused lesson topics will start to become clearer. That's exactly what you want. As you develop your essential questions, you want to be thinking: What questions naturally come up when studying this topic? And what questions need to be addressed and explored in order to cover this topic with depth and breadth?

Overall, guiding questions:

- Do not have a clear right answer.

- Raise additional questions that cross disciplines.

- Will remain relevant throughout the unit.

- Are designed to maintain interest throughout the unit.

- Are represented in multiple ways throughout the unit and constantly on view in the classroom.

- Help frame the culminating activity/assessment.

WHERE YOU ARE NOW:

Deciding on the lasting pieces of information for your unit is really coming up with what effect you want the unit to have on your students. In what ways do you want to challenge them to think and grow as learners? As you create these tools for your unit, you will start to see the pieces of the puzzle coming together. Once the lasting knowledge is in place and your guiding questions are organized in a way that develops knowledge and skill as needed, more and more lessons, topics, and skills will start to come to your head.

As you move through the next steps, use your lasting knowledge and guiding questions as the glue that brings your lessons together around your central theme. You've now moved from just a topic, to deciding what is valuable to your students about that topic; now you're ready to begin sorting out how to actually teach them about this idea in a way that's exciting and engaging.

PLANNING BACKWARD:

- Start with what you want your students to learn, then the goals of individual lessons, before eventually creating each lesson.

LASTING KNOWLEDGE:

- This is the big picture of your unit, where you decide what you are aiming to have your students understand by the culmination.

GUIDING QUESTIONS:

- Address the lasting knowledge, as well as skills and smaller pieces of knowledge that students will need in order to get to the lasting knowledge. They are the veins; lasting knowledge is the heart.

4

Structuring Your Unbound Unit

GUIDING QUESTION: *How do I ensure my students are getting the necessary information/skills from this unit?*

NOW THAT YOU HAVE A THEME, SOME LEARNING GOALS, AND A PLAN TO GUIDE STUDENTS TO THOSE UNDERSTANDINGS, IT'S TIME TO START CREATING YOUR UNIT! As we begin thinking about how to design the actual lessons and activities, we'll continue to plan backward, starting by talking about how to develop creative culminations. From there, we'll look at how to organize your scope and sequence, starting with what you need each lesson to focus on. Then we'll wrap up by discussing thoughtful ways to assess. Although some aspects of this chapter may be familiar, try to focus on the unique aspects of planning when you are developing a unit that spans disciplines. This process becomes a bit different when you are developing lessons that intertwine subjects that were previously disparate entities.

THINKING ABOUT YOUR UNIT

Before we delve too deeply into the process again, let's take a minute to remind ourselves why we're embarking on this process. As you create your lessons, try to break out of some of the established molds of what a lesson looks like. The "I do, We do, You do" models that give us quick and clear ways of teaching each lesson make our lives easier, and are often very successful, but are they truly engaging our students in thoughtful, creative mind work? When you're designing lessons, try to think about the ways a college student, or even a graduate student, might explore a topic in great depth.

Even if the fundamental topic is fascinating to your students, it's easy to bog them down with an overreliance on building content knowledge. Try to steer away from reading a packet and filling in worksheets and move more toward discussion circles and opportunities to present work. What are the skills your student is going to be expected to have in college? (This may seem a long way off for our kindergarten teachers, but if you've been doing this for a while, you know the feeling when you get that first email from a former student off to college that makes you say, "that was how long ago that you were struggling with multiplication in my class!") Yes, they'll need to take notes and write papers, but more than that, they'll need to be able to synthesize the information given to them and develop their own thoughts and ideas. During and after college, they'll be expected to innovate and then to present their newfound understandings to their peers.

Creating, innovating, presenting, and so forth are the skills that will engage your students. When you're tempted to print out a big packet of information and then test them a week later on how well they learned it, take a minute to think of other ways to expose them to content. Instead of giving them a map to look at and then asking them later what it shows, why not have the class come together and create their own massive map, with each student responsible for one small section where they can dive into the topography, weather, natural resources, and history of their little region? There are always more exciting ways to teach things, so make sure in this process that you are thinking outside of the ways you've done things in the past.

In this chapter, I'll focus on a journalism unit I developed for my third graders. I approached its creation by thinking about what I would need to do if I decided I wanted to create a newspaper of my own. It quickly becomes one of my favorite units because of the incredible work my students were able to produce year after year. When presented with real-world topics and issues, students rise to the occasion, delighted that they are welcomed into the curious world of life outside of school. This particular study seemed to be accessible to every student in so many ways; it's easily differentiated, and it gives them constant opportunities to chase their unique interests. Also, this unit can easily be used at any grade level, K–12. Prereading may be a challenge, but you can create an all-visual newspaper, or even a comic book, where everything is drawn! For upper-level teachers, creating a newspaper can absolutely speak to every discipline. It also addresses some of underaddressed needs of high schoolers—like learning to write about science and math, asking them to explain their thinking in disciplines that often feel more "right answer" oriented. Learning to analyze and review information and developing a strong understanding of what is going on in the world today are vitally important skills for high schoolers to focus on.

One of the reasons I developed this unit was I noticed that, with the Internet, kids (like adults) are struggling to recognize the difference between facts and opinions. The way that we consume information has changed drastically in the last 15 years. The Internet makes it easy to find only the news they seek out, never having to read about a topic in a larger context. Students are rarely experiencing the power of deep investigative journalism and learning the importance of the role of the press. As teachers, it's our responsibility to prepare our students for the world they will find themselves in as they grow into adults. Often that means helping them understand some of the important legacies of the world we're in right now. Journalism is a key form for this crucial work.

At the same time, journalism feels particularly useful because it encompasses so many skills my students will benefit from developing, such as writing practice and interviewing. Both writing and interviewing are also important social/emotional skills. Included, too, are the mathematical aspects of layout and sales and the critical reading skills needed to understand the complex stories journalists cover. Additionally, journalism asks for a constant link to history and an ability to cover a topic from multiple angles. One student could research a historical piece on the development of the Endangered Species Act, while another could look at the current state of local endangered species. They can work together to create an article about the relevance of this act today in their community. As we go through this chapter, I'll continually come back to this journalism unit because it serves as a great model of the endless possibilities of cross-disciplinary units and is also easily translatable for all grade-level teachers.

DEVELOPING THE CULMINATION

Once you have your lasting understandings sorted out, the next key to this process is to develop a strong culmination, a final presentation or activity. The key to this is to think of an authentic way the students can display what they've learned. A strong culmination needs to have three elements: (1) It needs to showcase student work, (2) encourage interaction, and (3) present a new but relevant challenge. This is a chance to assess what they learned from the unit, as well as guide their learning throughout the process, by creating a tangible end goal to go along with the skill and content goals you've set. The culmination is more than just a wrap-up of the unit; it needs to be exciting enough that students look forward to showing off their work, innovative enough that it challenges every student, and faithful enough that it is a true exploration of the topic.

The journalism unit culminated in the creation of a full newspaper and a "Newsies" presentation (Figures 4.1 and 4.2). Not only did the students develop an entire newspaper from start to finish, including laying it out, getting advertisers, and

FIGURE 4.1. Our first newspaper!

FIGURE 4.2. Students in their newsie outfits check out their product.

all the nitty-gritty beyond writing every article, but they also learned about the early days of print journalism in America, and dressed as newsies to hand out their newspaper around the school and to parents. Then they held a symposium on journalism, with parents as the invitees. In small groups, they had discussions about the future of print, the positives and negatives of getting all of your news online, and the role of investigative journalism in the age of the Internet. The students came up with all of these topics, based on our months of conversations.

The three crucial aspects of a culmination will help you think about how to create an event that engages your students in meaningful work. First, the culmination should showcase a large part of students' work in this unit, whether that's one item that took a large amount of work, like the newspaper, or many smaller pieces that came together over the course of the unit, like the interactive displays for the Chumash Museum. This dimension gives students an opportunity to show what they know, be proud of their work, and display it in a way that highlights how hard they have worked and how much they have learned. It allows them to take on the identity they've been testing out—becoming museum curators, journalists, explorers, new immigrants, or whatever suits your theme.

Second, the culmination needs to encourage interaction. Whether it's a discussion, public speaking, interactive activities, or something entirely different, the culmination should include activities that encourage students to interact with one another, as well as outsiders (parents, other students, other teachers) and share their learning. This attribute gives students an opportunity to teach what they've learned to others. Conversation requires students to synthesize their new understandings, internalizing them, and relating them to other topics and ideas. When they become teachers, they truly own their new knowledge and are able to think about it in new contexts.

Finally, the culmination should present a new but relevant challenge. The final piece should, in itself, allow the students to learn something new, with the process of the unit preparing them for the experience. For journalism, the creation of the newspaper was an additional concept, but the symposium was really what met the criterion of establishing something new. In the Chumash unit, this was the museum. It should always ask students to take their newfound knowledge and push it to the next level. This step allows the unit to connect to the outside world in yet another way. It challenges students to see how this information might be found or dealt with in the adult world. It also introduces them to things they may not otherwise participate in or get to have a hand in creating. Allowing them to take on the adult role in the creation of a museum, the organization of a symposium, or even the coordination of speakers, gives them a chance to take on responsibilities they are not usually afforded, which is not just exciting for them but crucial to developing skills for 21st-century learners.

Although you will know what the culminating event will focus on before you even begin the unit, this is also a space to allow students to innovate. Make sure that when you're designing the culmination, you have enough space for student opinions and ideas. If they have ideas of additional pieces or ways to push ideas further, they should feel they have a space to at least voice them, if not realize them. The culmination should ask them to own their newfound knowledge, and in doing so, it needs to feel to them like they had a say in what it looks like.

With the journalism unit, we brainstormed different ways we could get everyone talking about more than just our newspaper. I gave the students three options: a symposium with discussion topics, a speaker series where they each gave a brief speech and answered questions about a topic in journalism, or a panel discussion where they grouped together to present an idea and then hosted a discussion. They decided on the symposium, and then, in small groups, developed their topics. Although the topics may seem crazy for a third-grade classroom to come up with, the unit had been so carefully scaffolded that these were ideas the students had seen come up again and again, because they were all related to the guiding questions. In developing the symposium topics, they also displayed their ability to engage with the questions that drove the unit.

For upper-level teachers, the culmination can be entirely student designed. While I gave my students three options, you may just ask your students, "How do you want to share what you've learned" and tell them they need to put on an event that showcases their learning and asks them to think about this topic in a way that will engage others. For older students, this level of agency is not only empowering but a necessary skill for them to be developing. They are ready to be the leaders of their own projects and should find opportunities to guide their own learning and see their ideas come to fruition. Allowing this level of creativity in the classroom will also allow teenagers, who rarely feel at home anywhere, to find a place where they fit in the classroom, because it's something they've come up with themselves.

When you think about a culmination, go back to your lasting knowledge and think about ways that students can display their mastery. Below you'll find a list of possible ways to frame a culmination:

- Interactive museum

- Gallery showcase (Figure 4.3)

FIGURE 4.3. A student writes a Post-it on another student's work during a gallery walk.

- Poetry slam

- Symposium

- Panel discussions

- Plays

- Role playing (i.e., wax museum)

- Creating monuments or murals

- Design challenges

- Building models

- Inquiry challenge (ask their own questions about the topic and research it)

- Creating original music or pieces of writing

- Designing their own versions of a relevant building/sculpture

ORGANIZING THE SCOPE AND SEQUENCE

Before writing out the scope and sequence of my unbound unit, I like to go back to the lasting knowledge and think about those two outer rungs that encompass the skills needed to get to the final understandings: What information do the students need to have in order to get where I want them to go? For journalism, this was a long process. We started with current events at the beginning of the year. Every week, three students were responsible for bringing in a piece of local, national, or international news (Figure 4.4). We discussed each article in two ways—the topic and the writing structure. As we got more into writing structure, we started to discuss Who? What? Where? When? Why? How? As a class, we identified this information in the weekly articles. Then, once we really got into the unit, the students practiced doing this in two directions: (1) going through an article and writing down the answer to each according to said

FIGURE 4.4. Our current events wall began at the beginning of the year to build background knowledge for our journalism unit.

article and (2) taking a piece of information and writing down the answer to each (Figure 4.5).

In crafting the unit, I wrote a list of skills the students needed to have (broken down far more than the lasting understandings, these are the small tools students need to be able to create or

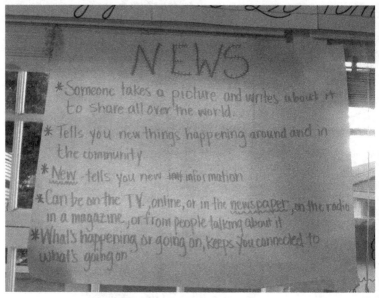

FIGURE 4.5. A chart from an early conversation about what "news" is.

engage with the topic), in order to create a newspaper article, with subpoints that could be specific lessons:

1. Understand what constitutes news

   • Recognize what is interesting to others

2. Understand the basic structure of an article

   • Introduction, information, analysis, conclusion

3. Familiarity with printed news

   • The structure, format, and look of a newspaper

   • Understand ancillary pieces, like book reviews and opinion sections

4. Understand the basic components of news

   • Who, what, where, when, why, and how

5. Have critical reading skills

   - Determine fact vs. opinion

   - Use context clues to understand challenging vocabulary

   - Underline key pieces of information

   - Reflect while reading

6. Be able to vary their writing style

   - Said is dead!

   - Use and set up quotations

7. Develop the interpersonal skills necessary to interview

   - Develop strong questions

   - Interview a classmate

   - Write the questions in advance, and practice writing quickly and legibly

Then I began thinking about the different ways to connect out to the other disciplines. In this stage, you're thinking: *What concrete ways can I use this lens to approach different/multiple subjects?*

1. Organize the layout

   a. Geometry and multiplication

      i. Multiplication (number of lines per page)

      ii. Geometry—spacial awareness and organization of shapes within a set area and perimeter

   b. Sales

      i. Cost analysis with different scenarios

      ii. Sell advertising space

      iii. Fundraise

c. History of journalism

    i. The start of printing

    ii. Early newspapers

       • Different newspapers for different demographics

    iii. The First Amendment

       • Freedom of speech and freedom of the press

With this outline, I now had a good sense of what every lesson needs to cover. The next step was to put them in order to build skills and knowledge. Then it can all be organized into a scope and sequence, with pauses for assessment and space to align the standards as lessons are built out. In Figure 4.6, you see what the scope and sequence for the natural disasters unit

1. Survey and Introduction **Objective:** Students will have an opportunity to shape the unit by sharing their prior knowledge and learning goals. Additionally, students will get an introduction to each feature. **Standard:**	2. 5 Forces of Nature **Objective:** Students will choose 3 Forces of Nature to explore more through centers and create an exploration map. **Homework:** students will draw on their maps the locations of the fault lines as well as volcanoes *2 days* **Standard:**	3. Critical Eye on Hurricanes **Objective:** Students will explore how forces of nature affect different places differently by looking at Hurricane Katrina's affects on New Orleans **Homework:** Students will add to their map the locations of Hurricanes **Vocabulary:** Basin **Standard:**	4. Critical Eye on Earthquakes **Objective:** Students will explore how forces of nature affect different places differently by looking at the Haitian earthquake and the recent earthquake in Japan. **Homework:** Students will add to their map the locations of Tornadoes **Vocabulary:** **Standard:**	5. Living in a Place With Earthquakes **Objective:** Students will do a shared writing activity to write a letter to students at a school in Japan to use what they have learned about earthquakes to ask how students prepare. **Homework:** Students will write individual letters to the students in Japan. **Vocabulary:** **Standard:**
6. Critical Eye on Tsunamis **Objective:** Students will look at controversies surrounding aide to countries after the 2004 Tsunami in the Indian Ocean. **Homework:** **Vocabulary:** **Standard:**	7. Critical Eye on Aide **Objective:** Students will look at the different aide that countries have received. They will draw conclusions about how aide is distributed to different countries. **Homework:** **Vocabulary:** **Standard:**	8. Debate on Aide **Objective:** Students will formulate an opinion regarding aide (Should countries have more preventative infrastructure? Should there be different amounts given to different countries?) And begin to write a persuasive essay, students will debate their points with a partner. **Homework:** **Vocabulary:** **Standard:**	9. Plan for the Future **Objective:** Students will pick a specific area that is vulnerable to a force of nature. They will write a persuasive essay choosing three points to help this area be prepared. **Homework:** **Vocabulary:** **Standard:**	

FIGURE 4.6. Sample scope and sequence.

looks like midway through the process. I had a good sense of many of the activities, but not all of the pieces are sorted out yet. Then, the completed one for journalism includes more lesson topics. The scope and sequence does not need to include the activity of the lesson, just the objective. From this, you'll build out each piece.

THOUGHTFUL ASSESSMENT

In these units, it's important to note that assessment can take on many forms. It's particularly valuable to constantly assess for misconceptions. As you'll be talking about a topic that students may have some background knowledge on, a thoughtful preassessment to find out what students already know will help you address misconceptions in the lessons and identify strengths the students already have. With the journalism unit, I started with a simple preassessment (Figure 4.7)—I asked the students to answer the question: *What is a journalist? What is a newspaper?* Then they filled in boxes about what they knew, what they thought, what they hoped, and what they wondered about our journalism unit. This is a simple way to get as much information as you can about what students already know about this topic. Additionally, make sure that your preassessment gives you an idea of what students are most curious about when it comes to this topic. You always want to be building off of their own curiosity, and the preassessment will help you determine exactly what that is. Whatever your preferred method of preassessment, this is an important first step.

From there, building in some thoughtful, creative assessments is particularly important. Large, open-ended questions, like the ones above, are a good place to start. Although this will yield a wide variety of answers, you can qualify the way the students answer in order to narrow the writing and show whether or not they're understanding. For example, you can ask that they use certain words you've used through the unit in the response in a way that demonstrates they understand the

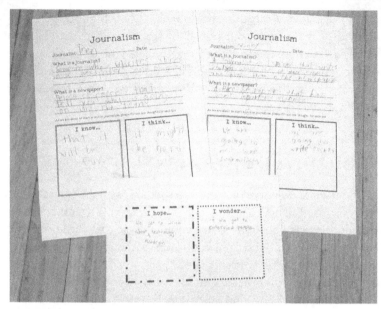

FIGURE 4.7. This simple preassessment gave me a sense of what students knew about journalism and what they were excited to learn.

meaning. Remember when evaluating student progress that assessments should also be multisensory and should not rely entirely on reading and writing skills. Verbal assessments are a great way to check in with students and get a clearer picture of their understandings, as it's not going to be affected by their reading/writing skills. Doing 5-minute conferences with each student at least two or three times through the unit is a crucial and important way to engage with students. I find scheduling six of these a day allows me to finish in a week and have a clear sense of where each student is.

Beyond check-ins and written assessments, you can construct a multitude of ways to build multimodal assessments. If you have access to technology, having students create brief podcasts on a topic is a great way to check in with their understandings. They can do a brief "talk" about a topic you give them and can be asked to include several important points. For the jazz unit, I had students create a brief podcast about one of the six musicians we learned about. They used their in-class notes and the books we'd read together, and created a brief talk that included several required elements (like date of birth, instrument played, favorite songs, and so forth). You can make a brief video on one of the important prerequisite knowledge topics and then have students discuss the video in small groups while you go between to listen to the conversations. Do turn-and-talks, have them each share one piece of interesting information from the video, or go share their newfound learning with a younger class. These types of activities all allow you to get a sense of where students' understandings are and aren't entirely contingent on reading/writing skills. You'll find that students who often struggle putting pen to paper will be more successful when given opportunities to express themselves verbally. Students need to be assessed in multiple ways, not only to show you the ways they learn and show their learning best, but so that they have opportunities to feel successful.

Additionally, students should be assessing themselves and asked to reflect on their work throughout the process. I always create a tracking sheet that students use to manage their own tasks. Figure 4.8 shows the journalism tracking sheet. As students move from one task to the next, they have to check in with me to make sure they're completing each properly and ready for the next. They also need to reflect on their work and discuss what they plan for the next step. This type of check is incredibly important to help students develop a strong internal compass for managing independent work. Helping elucidate the steps they need to take to reach the end goal, and building in time to pause and reflect, builds strong critical thinking skills.

Rubrics are another important tool to help build independent, critical thinking, and reflection, while also giving students the tools they need to be successful. They are a key tool to setting high expectations and giving students the support they need to achieve them. Small and large projects throughout the unit should have clear rubrics that make expectations explicit.

Tracking My Article's Progress

Dear Journalist,
As you work on your final article for our newspaper, please follow the steps on this tracker. When you complete a step, initial that box, and bring it to me to initial, along with the work you have done for that step. All of this hard work is going to create an amazing newspaper! Don't forget to use the resources on the bottom before coming to me for help. :)
Love,
Ms. Miro

Task	Reminders	My Initials *This means I know I have followed all directions and done my best work.*	Ms. Miro's Initials *Ms. Miro has checked my work and has given me permission to move on to the next step*
I have found a topic	- Fill out the topic organizer - Remember to think about a topic that is **dynamic** and **interesting**.		
My parents approve of my topic	- Bring home the parent approval sheet - Be sure to fill out "Why I chose this" and explain to your parents what excites you about this topic.		
My first interview is organized	- Fill out the first interview organizer - The first person you interview will be someone you know, that has knowledge of your topic - Make sure your questions are **thick**		
My second interview is organized	- Fill out the second interview organizer - The second person you interview will be someone you don't know, who has important knowledge about the topic - Remember to discuss with me the method you'll use for your interview (phone, email, etc…)		
I have completed my interviews	- Make sure you take **careful** and **accurate** notes during your interviews. - Be sure to say "thank you!" :)		
I have my 5 W's and H answered	- 5 W's and H: Who? What? Where? When? Why? How?		
I have organized my layout	- Create a layout for the pages using the instructions we discussed - Make sure your layout meets all of the requirements		
I am ready to start writing	- I have my outline complete, and I am confident I know exactly what I want to write - I have decided on a writing method that works best for me (typing, dictating, hand-writing…) - I have all of my materials organized and ready, including my favorite quotes from my interviews		

Before you come to me with a question, try these steps:
- Check in with your peer group before coming to me.
- Ask yourself what tools in the classroom can help you answer the question you have.

FIGURE 4.8. A rubric for journalism projects.

Students should always be asked to fill out a rubric with their own self-evaluation whenever a teacher fills one out. This activity is crucial to building their reflective thinking skills. It's easy at first to give yourself perfect marks on everything. Over time, when students recognize discrepancies between their self-evaluated rubric and the teacher-evaluated one, it will give them the opportunity to think more critically about their own performance. It helps them compartmentalize and assess each task, learn their own strengths and weaknesses, and address them, all without feeling like they've "failed." On the other hand, students who are too hard on themselves can learn to recognize that is equally futile. Building an accurate sense of their capabilities and output is critical to supporting students' emerging self-awareness.

Finally, the culmination should also act as a final assessment. If you need to, you can certainly create a traditional test that questions student knowledge of the content on which you have focused. Although the traditional test will give you a sense of a student's grasp of the material taught, without a thoughtful exercise, you will not be able to accurately assess the skills and process learned. With each culmination, I create at least one rubric for grading student's final work/participation. Often, there are multiple aspects to the rubric that cover a variety of pieces beyond content learned (Figure 4.8). Going this in-depth relates back to many of the UDL principles you've seen throughout this chapter. Giving students a wide variety of tasks to be assessed on ensures that struggles in reading and writing don't completely hinder their overall success. Students who struggle with writing still have many areas to be successful, and students who struggle with math do as well.

Overall, if you start with a strong preassessment that gives a clear sense of misconceptions, then build in multiple creative, open-ended assessments throughout, as well as check-ins and tools for accountability, like trackers and rubrics, at the end of the unit, you will have a very strong sense of where each of your student's understandings are, and you'll be able to adjust the unit as you go, in order to be as effective as possible.

With all of this structure carefully mapped out, you'll be ready for the fun part—designing the actual lessons. In the next chapter, we'll explore what that looks like, keeping the UDL Guidelines close at hand.

WHERE YOU ARE NOW:

Now that we're really into the meat of creating an unbound unit, continue to think outside of the box. Look around at ways that adults share information with one another for inspiration. Museums, symposiums, panels—these are all tools that students can use to share their newfound learning in creative and interactive ways (Figures 4.9 to 4.11). As you develop your stop and sequence, think about the smaller skills and tools students need in order to see the bigger picture. You're now really thinking about each lesson objective, without having to actually build the lessons just yet. Then, as you structure your scope and sequence in order to carefully scaffold learning, think about moments when you'll need to assess your students and get a clear sense of where they are. Traditional assessments like tests and quizzes can be used, but you may find more creative approaches will be more fruitful. Now that you've got this all put together, you're ready to build your lessons, and then get to teaching!

CULMINATIONS:

- Should be exciting, innovative, and faithful to the topic.

- They do this by:

  - Showcasing student work.

  - Encouraging interaction.

  - Presenting a new but relevant challenge.

DEVELOPING A SCOPE AND SEQUENCE:

- Use the list of skills you developed in Chapter 3 to start your list.

- Write out all of the skills your students need, paying attention to including multiple disciplines and ways of approaching the topic.

  - If you think of a lesson that could go with that, mark it down in your outline.

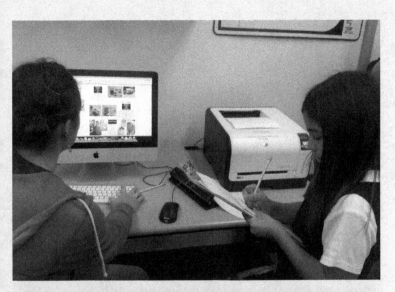

FIGURES 4.9 AND 4.10. A student interviewing and going over her notes.

FIGURE 4.11. A student sees her article in print!

- Assessment
    - Begin with a preassessment.
    - Assess consistently throughout the unit, being especially sure to check for misconceptions.
    - Creative assessments with big open-ended questions should be included throughout.
    - Don't rely on just written assessments; include verbal assessments, which can be creative, like asking students to create a podcast.
    - Conference often with students.
    - Use tracking documents and rubrics to help students have clear expectations and self-evaluate.

REMINDER ABOUT UDL:

- This is really the moment to check in with the UDL Guidelines and see where you need to be thinking about your diverse group of learners.

- Make sure that you're including a wide variety of topics that will reach students in a wide variety of ways.

- For examples, see Appendix A.

Unbound Is Variable: 5
Developing a Unit
for Every Student

> GUIDING QUESTION: *Are my lessons connecting ideas and information across disciplines while also taking into account the learning styles of all of my students?*

THE POWER OF AN UNBOUND UNIT IS FOUND IN ITS ABILITY TO REACH EVERY STUDENT IN YOUR CLASSROOM. As you've seen through earlier examples, like the student who created the 3D model of the village, if your unit reaches into the subject in a variety of ways, students will naturally find the pieces that speak to them the most. That is one of the great parts of these types of units: The students who love math but have not found their stride in writing will find activities that integrate the two and help strengthen one while using their interest in the other to fuel their intrigue. Although student interest is crucial to the strength of the unbound unit, in order to have true interest, the unit must be accessible for all of your students. This is why an Unbound Classroom fits so well with UDL. One of the fundamental goals of an unbound unit is to ensure that every student in your classroom is learning and growing. As the tenets of UDL help us understand, this requires knowing your students well enough to anticipate their challenges. It also means that as you're developing lessons, you're thinking about all of the different ways you can engage your students.

In addition, as you create groups for your students, you'll find opportunities to differentiate instruction in a way that brings each student to similar outcomes but allows them to go through the process in different ways. As you read through this chapter, you'll find quite a few concrete lesson ideas, but more than that, the chapter is meant to help you create a mind-set while planning—one that uses your creative skills to think about every student in your classroom.

THREE WAYS TO THINK ABOUT VARIATION

In this chapter, we'll look at three pieces to creating lessons that reach every student: (1) making flexible options for representation, action and expression, and engagement; (2) creative integration; and (3) starting with an activity that builds background knowledge and interest while remaining accessible and exciting. We'll start by talking about how to differentiate instruction in your unbound unit. One of the most important pieces to keep in mind during this work is that in order for these units to work well, lessons need to be structured in a way that allows all learners to engage with the topic. That may look different for different students, but there need to be ways that each student can become their own type of expert on the topic. This will be the meat of the first section of this chapter, how to design creative lessons, especially how to think about differentiation in your planning. Then, we'll talk about creating a lead-in activity. This is an initial project that introduces students to the topic and allows you to assess their background knowledge. Lastly, we'll talk about how to think creatively about integrating the disciplines.

Throughout this chapter, I will try to give you straightforward ideas for how to craft your lessons, but the reality is that this is a part of the process that will rely a lot on your own creativity. This is the time to put yourself in the shoes of your students. You are about to study an entirely new topic (and really the first time you create one of these units, that's just what you're doing!). What does that process look like? What are you interested in learning? What would be an engaging way to learn about this topic? If you need your students to understand how engineers test different materials to build with, have them test out some materials you can easily find. You can make things open-ended—everyone gets two cups of sand, and anything they can find in the classroom; the goal is to create a block that can hold weight. Create an engineer's notebook organizer to go with it that asks students to brainstorm ideas, test, record their findings, and so forth. Although the lessons are more focused on the K–6 teacher, our upper-level teachers will find that these ideas and lessons are easily translatable for older students and more complex topics. For this chapter, I'll continue to use the journalism unit as an example because it is such a trove of resources when it comes to thinking about how to design the unit and its lessons.

PLANNING TO CREATE OPTIONS IN INSTRUCTION

A question I often encounter when helping teachers through this process for the first time is: How do I provide options in my teaching and for student performance when I need every student to accomplish the goals of the unit? This is a crucial aspect of why this topic is so relevant for those of us working to integrate UDL into the classroom. If you craft your unit carefully, with a wide variety of ways for students to engage in the topic, you will find that while every lesson may not speak to every child, the level of excitement about the topic will project itself and help keep students engaged. Then this engagement needs to be capitalized on in order to carefully scaffold and address the individual needs of students. Although many of the smaller day-to-day projects will need a single mini-lesson to start, creating varied levels within the activity, especially those with small group work, is an accessible way to begin differentiating your methods and materials.

You can easily integrate different activities into groups already in place in your classroom. For example, in reading groups, we created a book review for our newspaper with our guided reading books. My strongest readers were given 10 reviews of varying types and asked to come up with a list of 10 essential elements of a good book review. They were then challenged to each write their own review of the book, and then come together and take pieces of each to create a collaborative article.

In contrast, my struggling readers started out reading one book review of our last book at every meeting for a week. Then together we generated a list of important parts of a review and created a graphic organizer that outlined the structure of a book review. Together, they filled in all of the important pieces for their current book, and then we worked on transitions and other important elements they needed extra practice with and put it all together for a great book review. In the end, both groups had fantastic book reviews printed in our newspaper, and a reader wouldn't be able to tell the difference in their writing skills, but the process to get each one there looked very different and addressed different needs and skills, while keeping each working at their highest potential.

A key to success is to make varied groups a staple of your classroom. Varying your student groups means that you don't always group based on skill level, and if you do group based on skill, you assess and adjust frequently. I varied my math groups every day based on strengths and weaknesses in relation to the topic rather than math overall. For each unit, I began with a preassessment directly linked to each math lesson; then, based on performance on the preassessment and my knowledge of the students, I adjusted the groups every day based on their understanding of the topic. For example, in a geometry unit where we began with perimeter, went through area, and then started volume, I began with a pretest that was two questions from each lesson

I was planning to teach, as well as some ancillary questions that covered underlying skills students needed, like multiplication of three numbers. Then I would plan each lesson with groups doing slight variations of the same activity. Usually the minilesson was the same, but the activities were different.

Although you would think that this would consistently put students in the same groups (strong mathematicians, on track, and struggling), it revealed far more than that and gave me enough information to vary groupings. There was a group that confused area and perimeter, and their activities were focused on understanding the differences; there was a group that understood it all well, though some needed help with math facts, so they were often in another group that needed to work on multiplication. There were students who struggled, but they were often placed in groups or partnerships with students who had a slightly stronger grasp of the topic. I made all of the groupings in advance so that I could see that they were constantly changing. This eliminated "cliques," separating strong math performers from struggling ones. Then, when we encountered challenging, open-ended math questions, each group could have different numbers to work with without much sense that some were easier to manipulate than others.

This is the same idea you want to include in your unbound unit. As you create partnerships and groups, make sure that you are varying them every time. That way, when there are times when it really needs to be based on where students are, you are able to group that way without students feeling that one group is stronger than another. The idea is to make partner work and group work so common in the classroom that students are used to working with everyone. Yes, they may have some sense of students being stronger at certain subjects, but because your unbound unit isn't focused in a certain subject, it challenges their assumptions about one another. When students doing an activity that includes some math, some reading, and some writing, they focus less on who is "the best" at math or writing or reading. The focus becomes the lesson goal. This way every student feels comfortable learning at his or her own pace.

From there, I add or subtract learning supports so that students who need more challenge or struggling ones who need less can stay engaged. The Chumash Museum economists, for example, had quite a few additional tasks they had to cover. Although it seemed to each group that that was just based on the topic they had chosen, it was really because they were all strong mathematicians who needed additional challenges. For journalism, the strongest writers contributed extra articles, completed more interviews, and were challenged to make their topics more specific in order to require more research.

Planning for 25 to 30 variable students can certainly be overwhelming. That is why the structure of the unit and the culmination should help make this task far easier. Think about the goals you have for the unit, and then as you work through each task with the students, it will become clear what additional tools they each need. Some may need a specific lesson on a skill (maybe they struggle with multiplication, or writing in complete sentences), while others may need a more challenging task (they may be able to finish the activity in just a few minutes and need a more complex activity). As long as that end result is sufficiently unique to each student or group, it will become much easier to adjust teaching in small ways to ensure each student gets what they need in order to become their own version of "experts" on the topic and meet the goals of the unit.

CREATING A LEAD-IN PROJECT

When you start actually designing the lessons, go to your scope and sequence and see how you've decided to build skills and knowledge. If this is not the first unit you'll teach for the school year, it can be a great opportunity to create a lead-in project that you start at the beginning of the year and builds at least one of the skills you need students to have.

For journalism, we started weekly current events at the beginning of the school year. Each week, three students brought in a piece of local, national, or international news. By the time we started the unit after winter break, each student had brought in one of each type, and everyone was familiar with newspapers and the act of reading a newspaper article. We would discuss each article, not just the topic, but the construction of the article and the writing style. Students might work in pairs or groups (Figure 5.1). With just 10–20 minutes once a week, we'd laid a strong foundation for the work ahead. This activity helped students build their own background knowledge. It also helped me identify and address misconceptions before we even got close to the unit.

We had natural opportunities to talk about fact vs. opinion, reliable sources of information, strong vs. weak writing styles, persuasive writing and opinions, all while working with our lead-in activity. Additionally, this helped build a context for the unit and

FIGURE 5.1. Students working together to figure out the pieces of an article.

make the study relevant. By the time the students were creating their own newspaper, they had learned to value news and newspapers as an important way of getting information about what is happening in their community, country, and world.

This lead-in also allowed me to address the differing needs of some of my students. Some students were allowed to listen to news articles. If they struggled significantly with reading or visual processing, we would find the article in audio and print. Some students would look to more kid-centered news sources like *Time for Kids* and *Scholastic News*, while others were pulling from the *New York Times* and *Washington Post*. From the beginning, the lead-in activity:

- Built interest and background knowledge in the subject.

- Laid a contextual foundation for the study.

- Helped me address misconceptions and issues that came up.

- Allowed me to vary the work based on the needs of my students.

In all, you want a lead-in activity that checks all of these boxes. With journalism, this was an easier one to create because current events are a common classroom practice. Other themes may require less traditional activities, but no matter what they should try to create excitement and give you some useful feedback.

There are many ways to create a strong lead-in activity depending on your unit. For example, a unit on immigration could mean that each week a different student is asked to interview someone they know who immigrated (or the child of someone who immigrated) and do a brief presentation, each covering the same critical questions, in order to highlight the diversity of experience. This lead-in could integrate home in some way, if possible, in order to bring the students' lives into the classroom and the unit and build their personal connection to the theme before they begin. A unit about another country could include an around-the-world journal, sent at the start of the year to someone in a different country, with information about each student, that asks them to then send the journal on to someone else in a different country.

If there's not a clear way to create a lead-in, consider a book bag project (Figure 5.2) where you send home a book and activity to do with a family member or friend. This can be a great way to introduce a topic slowly over the course of a few weeks before you start the unit. A book bag project should include an engaging and relevant picture book for younger learners, a newspaper article or short story for older students, along with a family response journal and student response journal. Be sure to make your book bag multisensory. If possible, an old iPod can be used to share a recording of you reading the book. Activities should be sent

FIGURE 5.2. The pieces of a book bag project with *Wangari's Trees of Peace*.

home in all relevant languages, in order to make family participation as easy as possible. Integrating families is fantastic, but be sure to be sensitive to family dynamics and needs.

The student response journal asks a few questions about the book and topic, and also encourages a brief discussion with a family member or friend about the book (e.g., For *Wangari's Trees of Peace* I asked: What did the person you read the book with think about Wangari Maathai's work planting trees?). Then the family response journal just asks the family member to reflect on the experience of reading with the child and also asks for their thoughts on the topic. You can even include an activity that relates to what's to come.

A book bag project is also a great lead-in activity if you are having trouble coming up with something that feels relevant to the theme you've picked. If you have a great book on the topic, consider trying this. For older grades, a project where students bring home a brief piece of writing, maybe a poem, short story, or song, which they read/listen to with a family member or friend and then both respond, can have the same affect. Tying the activity to the student's home life helps them see relevance in the topic and also begins a conversation at home about the theme. Once you've done an activity like this, it is more likely that a parent will ask, "How is that study about eminent people going?" Or "What are you learning about jazz now?" These are the kinds of questions that will allow students to demonstrate their newfound expertise and feel proud of being able to share information that their families will find relevant and interesting.

THINKING CREATIVELY ABOUT INTEGRATION

Once you've designed your lead-in, look at what other skills you need to teach, and start thinking about the most effective, but also most inclusive and interesting way, to teach each skill. For example, it will be easy to integrate math by creating worksheets with word problems about the topic. It might be more interesting, valuable, and complex to students if you ask them to identify the mathematical and logical reasoning skills involved in the topic and how to teach them.

For journalism, we discussed how to design each page of the newspaper. The students were given a challenge: We have a page that's 8.5 inches × 17 inches. We need to fit as much text as possible, while keeping 1/4-inch margins (meaning they had to remeasure the dimensions). All text must be 12-point Times New Roman; the average word will then be 0.2 inches. How would you design your page? In these kinds of activities, the teacher needs to be actively conferring with students, and groups should be made carefully in order to ensure not just success but comprehension and collaboration. It can also tie to your traditional curriculum. Before doing this lesson, we worked through three lessons about measurement and area in our standard math curriculum, ensuring the measuring, area, and perimeter skills the students needed were there, and also getting in some required lessons before jumping into the more complex. If you have a curriculum you need to work with, you can absolutely find ways to integrate it into your thematic study.

When you start thinking of lessons, consider beginning with ones that fit within a discipline and within the theme, like the one above. This is already a change to the way most of us were trained to think about teaching. At first, it may be hard to find connections to every discipline, but I promise, they exist. As you begin to find them, branching out to larger questions and connections will become clearer. A unit on Islam could have a lesson on Muslim art, including tessellations and symmetry lessons as a math piece. That lesson actually transcends the disciplines, connecting art and math in a way children rarely get to see. A unit on lions could look at the change in the amount of habitat lions have had over time. Then by doing a lesson on rates and ratios, students could try to figure out how much space one lion typically lives in, in order to see how much land is needed to sustain or grow current lion populations.

Again, this transdisciplinary lesson has them thinking about ecology, environment, spatial awareness, rates and ratios, conservation, the history of land use, public vs. private land, and so forth. So many other conversations can become a part of this lesson—it's up to you where you take it.

The key is to think about the many aspects of the topic you've picked. If you've picked a great lens, it will be inherently multifaceted. When planning lessons, go back to that initial research you did, and see where you might be able to make connections. Your lasting knowledge should also help guide you to these types of activities, as well as the scope and sequence. Once you've gotten your lesson topics figured out, and you've ensured connection across all of the disciplines, there are some critical elements to keep in mind in order to ensure that all of your learners' needs are met.

WHERE YOU ARE NOW:

Now your unit is mapped out, and you've got a sense of how to design each lesson. You may be thinking at this point: What do my lessons actually look like? This is the part that we've built toward, but that is really in your hands. Now you have the tools to create innovative, creative, integrated lessons that reach every student in your classroom.

PLANFUL VARIATION IN TEACHING AND LEARNING:

- Rotate groups consistently.

- Bring students to the same end by adjusting the activities to make them accessible for all.

- Start with your lowest students and add challenges for students who are ready for them.

LEAD-IN ACTIVITY:

- Builds necessary skills

- Builds background knowledge

- Checks for misconceptions

- Creates intrigue and highlights relevance and value

CREATING INTEGRATED LESSONS:

- Think about the ways a topic is approached in the world.

    - How does a journalist encounter math?

    - How does a jazz musician use math?

    - How is math relevant to understanding the changing habitat of lions?

- Incorporate real-world activities.

    - Interviewing, podcasting, measuring, designing, etc.

Fostering the Culture of an Unbound Classroom

6

GUIDING QUESTION: *How does it feel to be a learner in an Unbound Classroom?*

THE CULTURE OF YOUR CLASSROOM COMMUNITY IS AN INTEGRAL PIECE OF SUCCESSFULLY UNBINDING YOUR CLASSROOM. In this chapter, I will take you through the unit I always use to start the year it seems appropriate, with all of this backward work, to end where I begin!: a study of people who made a difference for their community. I use this unit at the beginning of the school year because it allows for many moments to develop a constructive, supportive classroom culture, as well as introduce the type of cross-disciplinary thinking students will be asked to do throughout the year. My students become accustomed to hearing my feedback, recognizing it as valuable (not judgmental) and positively impacting their final project in a way that was concrete. As you think of finally executing the unit, bringing the entire process together, keep in mind four key elements:

- Students must, first and foremost, recognize the value of cross-disciplinary work. The topic must be engaging, and furthermore it must be connected to the outside world in a way that creates intrigue and excitement. Students' curiosity must be involved.

- Second, the classroom community needs to welcome diverse learning styles. Students will be doing different activities at different paces and in different ways, and they must feel that this variability is an everyday part of the classroom, not that they are somehow different or worse because their process looks different.

- Third, the majority of students must be able to do independent work and exploration. Unbound Classroom units are more challenging but still possible in the youngest grades where independent work is difficult. The amount of scaffolding and guided instruction will vary based on age and developmental stages, but students should be expected to and given opportunities to explore their individual interests.

- To that end, the fourth component is that students need to feel supported, and they need to know what you expect of them. If your students are afraid that they're going to get something wrong and get in trouble, this entire exercise will be a recipe for anxiety. There has to be a welcoming of failure, a clear sense that as the teacher you are not there to judge their every move but to support them in the ups and downs of their learning journey.

With these four elements in place, the classroom community will welcome the opportunity to challenge themselves and think outside of the normal box of school.

BUILDING YOUR COMMUNITY

In this chapter, we'll explore the four keys to creating a classroom environment that is ready for interdisciplinary work. The example unit I'll discuss in this chapter is one I like to begin the year with: people who made a difference in their community.

For this unit, we began with a lead-in book bag project using *Wangari's Trees of Peace,* a book about Nobel Laureate Wangari Maathai's work planting trees. Because we started the year with this unit, the book bag began the first week of school and went through the first week of the unit. In class, we began by studying leaders of the civil rights movement. We created a human monument to Rosa Parks. In groups, they decided on an important moment in Rosa Park's life and then "became" a monument by getting into various positions. For example, one group re-created the scene on the bus, with Rosa refusing to give up her seat and a white passenger standing over her, while all the other passengers look on with worry and anger. They got into position and each "broke out" of the monument to explain their role.

Then students were challenged, with the help of several books, to see beyond the "rose-colored glasses" version of each person and explore their lives in more (age-appropriate) depth. We talked about how each of these people were humans who made mistakes but also made choices that required a tremendous amount of courage. Humanizing the people you teach about is crucial. If the heroes students read about never make mistakes, how will your students ever see themselves making a difference if they feel their fallibility makes them unlike any consequential person they've read about?

We then studied the ways that communities honor those who've impacted them. I started developing this unit while I was teaching at a school in a neighborhood that was entirely concrete, with the only color coming from graffiti and store signs. After walking past a huge mural that honored several community leaders, I decided to link what was essentially a biography unit to a study of public art forms as a way to honor those who make an impact on their community. Students eventually picked their own person to study from a long list of diverse names they rarely, if ever, came into contact with. They then researched the person and designed, then created, a 4-foot-by-2-foot mural that honored that person by depicting important moments in

FIGURE 6.1. Students' final murals in our "eminent people" unit.

their life (Figure 6.1). The unit culminated with a gallery walk around the school where the murals were displayed on the outside walls, and each student gave a 2-minute speech on their eminent person.

I started the school year with this unit for a few reasons. The first is that it got students into the work of school without going too deep into challenging skills right at the start. The lessons are accessible and engaging, and the unit itself can be completed in about a month. This unit also has a tremendous number of preassessments built into it that helped me get to know my students' strengths and weaknesses:

- There were math challenges where they had to organize their mural by calculating the area and perimeter of different aspects of their drawings. We walked down the street and measured different parts of the mural. We calculated ages and created a massive time line of the many people we studied.

- We wrote about people we read about, providing a strong example of their responses to nonfiction literature as well as contextual reading assessments (a reading assessment done outside of a formal testing system). We wrote stories of imaginary heroes, which displayed their creative writing skills.

- All of these activities gave me great insight into my students' processing, skill, and content knowledge and ability.

Additionally, this unit sets a great tone for the school year, with a mix of group and independent work, and a culmination that is lower-pressure and allows all students to find their voice, while also showcasing their work in a way that they haven't done before, and that gives them a lot of pride. Just the size of the mural alone is something particularly exciting to students, even those intimidated by art, because it is not about what it looks like—it is about finding ways to display the life of a person with only visuals.

KEY ONE: FINDING COMFORT IN CROSS-DISCIPLINARY WORK

Starting with an exciting unit that allows each student to pick their own topic is a great way to help students find joy in this type of open-ended work. This is the first key to creating the culture of your Unbound Classroom community. Students must recognize the value in studying all subjects through a particular theme and grow comfortable with this way of thinking. After we did a math unit exploring the ways a graffiti artist or painter can map out a painting using a grid system (Figure 6.2), a student asked me when we would have math today. When I responded that that was the math lesson for the day, she was flabbergasted! She replied, "Math has never felt like that for me. Usually I'm scared that I won't understand and won't be able to do it, but I didn't even notice we were doing math because I was so excited about measuring and mapping out my person!"

FIGURE 6.2. Students measuring outside for a mural math unit.

Activities like this—ones that integrate the theme seamlessly across disciplines, so that students aren't even thinking about what subject they are in—allow their preconceived subject-based worry to float away and give them a lens for exploring the work of the discipline in a new way.

Even if you don't begin with a full unit, having a few lessons that integrate disciplines through a single theme is a great way to begin the year with opportunities for exploration and success. You could take your school mascot and do a 3-day unit on the animal itself, the origin of the mascot in general, and some history of how the school picked the mascot. A math lesson about the distance the animal can travel, or its migratory patterns, can lead into a writing exercise about what it must be like to live as that animal, which can in turn connect to a read-aloud with a picture book about the animal, and then a study of where the animal population is now, what environmental factors influence its life today, and finally, a brief exploration of the history of the animal as it relates to the school. It all could culminate in a collectively written spoken word poem (each student has two lines about different topic) about the mascot, and voila! You've got a great starting unit that won't take up too much time but allows the students to begin to think thematically instead of disciplinarily. Your units, especially the first one, should be designed in a way that supports students feeling comfortable with unbound learning. By connecting a simple topic like the school mascot across the disciplines, and actively telling students that they are going to study this in a new and exciting way, they will grow comfortable and excited about learning in their Unbound Classroom.

KEY TWO: WELCOMING DIVERSE LEARNING

The next important component to creating an Unbound Classroom community is ensuring that your classroom welcomes diverse learning. In the first days of school, I always like to do an activity where we talk very explicitly about how we all learn in different ways. I ask the students what tools help them learn and what hurts their learning. They complete little forms on their own, then come back and share what they wrote. Often, conflicting information will help them recognize the small ways in which they approach learning differently. Inevitably, one student will say he learns better in a quiet environment, while another will say she does better when there's noise and activity around her. Take one of these points and open up a discussion about learning environments: Is one right and one wrong? If not, what does this tell us about the ways we learn? We all learn in different ways!

Throughout this conversation, I make a list of practices that students said help them learn on a chart (Figure 6.3). We keep that chart next to the classroom compact for the entire year and often revisit it when students need a reminder that we all need different things in order to feel successful. We also

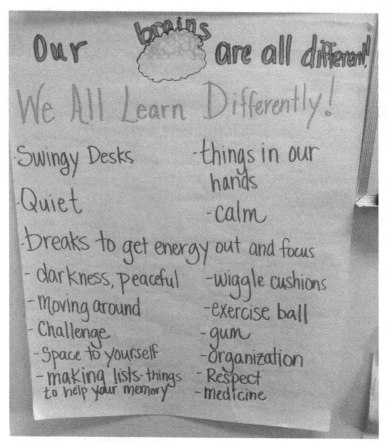

FIGURE 6.3. The chart we create in the first days of school about the different tools that help us learn.

talk about what success looks like and how that is different to different people. As they see the differences between themselves and their classmates, and feel comfortable sharing, not just in spite of those differences, but because they feel proud to say something different from the rest of their classmates, it furthers their sense that there's nothing wrong with needing something different from your classmate to help you learn best.

Additionally, early on, try to create a wide variety of groupings and pairings in all subjects. Just like we explored in Chapter 5, grouping is crucial. Don't immediately settle into reading groups and math groups and just stick to them for the next few months. Foster the belief that groups are made for a number of reasons, not just based on ability. In the public art unit, I had three groups for the human monument, students worked in groups of three to support one another in their mural planning (another great way to build accountability, communication, and collaboration—assigning small peer groups to discuss their work and their progress throughout the unit). They had small groups for each integrated math lesson. They also worked initially in groups of four to learn about a specific person in the civil rights movement and give a brief talk, as well as create a human monument, for each one. Every group for this was different, and I very consciously tried to ensure that every student was in a group with every other student at some point. Throughout the year, I changed groups constantly (math every day, reading every month or so, and so forth) so that students never felt set in the sense of where they were in the classroom, but also so that they learned to work with students who thought differently, behaved differently, and needed different things in order to succeed. Just as the units themselves reflect the real world, the experience should allow students to safely encounter the challenges of the real world, with one of the biggest being working with those who think differently from you.

KEY THREE: INDEPENDENCE

The third component—supporting independence—can be particularly challenging depending on your students. It is tempting to think of independence as a student's ability to work alone on a worksheet at their desk. This is not independence. Independence relies on students' abilities to think on their own, make decisions that will impact the success of their work, and adequately reflect on their own abilities. More practically, students need to be able to think of ways to creatively display the life of a person, without coming to ask you every 5 minutes if they can include a banana because Jane Goodall worked with primates. Getting your students to independence requires careful scaffolding, balanced support, and conscious confidence building on the part of the teacher. If the activities are scaffolded well, students will feel they have the tools to make their own decisions. If they have balanced support, they will have a good sense of when they should ask a teacher and when they should make their own decisions. If they have explicitly worked on building their confidence and belief in their own abilities, they will be able to sort through the dilemmas they may face.

You can use some very practical policies to help you build student independence. First, the peer support group is a great tool to help students develop confidence, while still having a sounding board in case of questions. With the creation of the mural, I didn't allow any student questions about what should or shouldn't be included in the mural. The students had a rubric (Figure 6.4) to help guide them and we went over (and wrote on a chart) attributes that would be inappropriate and those that would be appropriate. We had a brief lesson on the word "relevant," and on the rubric, students were guided to ask themselves if they weren't sure: "Is this relevant? Is it valuable to show the most important aspects of this person's life?"

Doing an activity like this at the start of the year is challenging to students who are used to having a clear right and wrong and being able to ask the teacher if they are right or wrong at any point. The rubric is the scaffold—they can look at it anytime to get similar feedback as they would get from me, but instead of having the soothing response of the teacher, they need to internally go through this process. This helps not only build comfort in doing tasks with no clear right answer but also confidence by supporting their ability to reflect.

Giving your students the tools to develop their own inner voice, one which is guiding, supportive, and reflective, as

HONORING THOSE WHO HAVE MADE A DIFFERENCE...
MURALS, MONUMENTS, MEMORIALS AND STATUES CULMINATION

ARTIST: _____ DATE: _____

HONORING: _____

CATEGORY	SCORE AND COMMENTS
SPEECH CONTENT - The person's name - The date the person was born - The date the person died - How the person died - Why was he/she important? - At least three important details - Explains the drawing thoroughly	
MURAL, MONUMENT, MEMORIAL OR STATUE - Clearly shows the person - Has details that are relevant to the person's life - Is neat - Clearly states the person's name - Includes at least one detail about the person's life - Is thoughtfully composed	
PRESENTATION - Makes eye contact with the audience - Face is clear the whole time (not holding your speech up in front of your face) - Speech is clear - Speech is loud enough that everyone can hear - Is within the three minute time constraint	

ADDITIONAL COMMENTS:

FIGURE 6.4. The murals rubric.

opposed to overly disparaging, or overly inflating, is one of the most crucial tools you can give your students. When you're thinking about how to build independence and confidence, think about what tools the students need in order to be successful at this task without your feedback, no matter what bumps they run into. When they do seek your feedback, ask them to reflect instead of giving them your opinion. "Do you feel you've met all of the criteria in the rubric?" If you know they're missing one piece, you can instruct them to go back and be sure they've met the requirements for that part. But beyond that, hold back on the urge to tell them how they are doing when they're in the midst of a project.

KEY FOUR: SUPPORT AND EXPECTATIONS

This leads into the last component. Students need to feel supported, and they need to know what is expected of them. I group these together because I think that while as teachers, we often talk about expectations, we spend less time talking about what the support looks like that helps students reach those expectations. We've delved into scaffolding. We've gone through tools like rubrics that help make expectations clear. All of these are crucial aspects to this final point. The overall idea behind this component though is a much more general feeling of support. The students need to feel that they are in a safe space, where they are known as individuals. These units cannot work unless you truly know your students. You need to be able to anticipate where each student will struggle, and where they will find success, in order to ensure a healthy balance of both. In turn, the students need to feel that you know them well enough that you would not be asking them to do something they cannot do. This trust is crucial because you are challenging your students to take on complex ideas. They need to know that you're not throwing them into something they're not ready for, because they will inevitably feel that worry and doubt. If they trust you, the moment will pass. They will realize they can do it, and it will reinforce their knowledge that you know and support them. This doesn't mean making lessons so simple that everyone feels great on everything. It means that when you have students who can't sit still for more than 10 minutes and struggle with reading, have them switch reading activities (and tables) every 10 minutes. You can't take a student to their edge and push the bounds of their knowledge and ability, if they don't let you.

WHERE YOU ARE NOW:

You are ready to build your unbound unit! You've got your topic selected, your lasting information and guiding questions mapped out, and your scope and sequence developed with a careful eye to building skills in many different ways. You've started construction of each lesson, thinking carefully about how to reach every learner, and now you've created supportive tools for your classroom that help build an inclusive, inquisitive classroom community that is ready for interdisciplinary work. You are ready to build your own Unbound Classroom!

THE FOUR KEYS TO A CLASSROOM COMMUNITY READY FOR CROSS-DISCIPLINARY WORK:

- Students must, first and foremost, recognize the value of cross-disciplinary work and feel comfortable with open-ended tasks.

  - Engaging topics connected to the outside world

  - Incites curiosity

- The classroom community needs to welcome diverse learning styles.

- The majority of students must be able to do independent work and exploration.

  - Requires careful scaffolding

- Students need to feel supported, and they need to know what you expect of them.

Final Thoughts

LUCIEN, MY DJING NEPHEW, IS NOW IN HIGH SCHOOL, AND I ASKED HIM ABOUT THAT TIME HE DJ'ED HIS THIRD BIRTHDAY PARTY. I guessed that he wouldn't even remember it. I certainly don't remember my third birthday. He laughed, a big, all-knowing teenager laugh, and said, "Oh yeah, that was so much fun. I love that Bad Brains song I played before we had cake." I certainly didn't expect that level of memory. I didn't remember what he played before cake. I didn't remember the cake (and I really love cake). I was too floored watching that tiny person do something I couldn't imagine how to do. He went on to tell me he's been working on learning the drum line in one of the songs he played at that birthday party, and how it's always been one of his favorites. I asked him how he knew which record was which when he was that little and couldn't read, and he said, "I have no idea."

The reality is that Lucien didn't remember how he did any of it. To him, it wasn't about the skill; he had the skill. It was about the experience. That's what created the lasting memory; that's what had value to him. In that moment, he had agency, he had choice, and he wasn't held back by his age or any inability. He was able to share his knowledge and skills with the people he loved, he was able to feel proud and capable, and he was only 3.

Imagine a world where every child gets to feel like a capable being from the time they are little. Imagine further, a classroom that empowers every student to pursue their interests, to travel the paths of their curiosity, to allow learning to be a natural process. What do our students look like at the end of this experience? The hope is that we create fearless, passionate learners who pursue their interests with fervor, don't shy away from situations, questions, or new information that is challenging, and understand the ways that their learning has helped them grapple with the world they live in. Maybe they don't know every fact about the American Revolution, but they may understand the intricacies of the relationship between a king and subjects in a distant land. They might not be able to restate every word of the Bill of Rights, but they can discuss the challenges that begin when we start assigning value to human beings, deeming some lesser and others greater. They may see the long-term implications of slavery and be able to look at what they see going on in their world right now as a further repercussion of dehumanizing human beings for so long. The goal is to foster students who are able to look at the big pictures in the world around them and ask insightful questions. The goal is to create critical thinkers, able to engage in the troubles that will face an always unpredictable future. The goal is to enable students to find themselves in their learning. Along the way, they will learn the content and the skills they need to be successful in college, in jobs, and in life.

Is that a tremendous goal? Absolutely. It is the fundamental goal of educators to enlighten the beings that come through their classroom, and therefore it is our great responsibility to find the best ways to do that. I hope that as you've gone through this book, a lightbulb has gone on a few times, and you've started to become inspired to integrate some of these ideas into your classroom. It's my hope that now you will have the tools to see the power of learning in a classroom that is not bound by the strictures of disciplines. Instead, you are empowered, challenged even, to think about what your students would enjoy learning and what they should be learning. When I looked at the graffiti around my students' neighborhood, mixed with powerful murals that were likely done with little government approval, but community support, I thought about the ways that my students interact with art. They weren't kids whose parents dragged them to museums, they were kids who watched their siblings, or cousins, or friends take out a spray paint can and write a tag on a wall or do a quick doodle as a way of taking ownership over some public space. Their art was the giant murals on the bodega wall, and when I talked about art as paintings in museums and sculptures in foreign countries, art was something distant, irrelevant, existing in a world that didn't recognize them. In turn, school didn't recognize them, their world, their art. Creating a unit that welcomes their world into the classroom and asks them to think critically about it makes school a place that is welcoming to who they are. It is no longer foreign, distant, and useless. Suddenly, it is helping them understand what's going on around them.

Think back to the little kid saying, "Why?" And welcome that curiosity into the classroom. Help them find the answers to questions relevant to their world, and in turn, teach them how to ask questions about the greater space around them. Eventually, your intrepid explorers will be ready to question, wonder, and adventure in the world on their own. They will have a toolbox filled with skills they need and a mind ready for anything that comes their way.

Appendix A
Designing With the
UDL Guidelines in Mind

THE UDL GUIDELINES ARE A GREAT TOOL WHEN IT COMES TO DESIGNING LESSONS. Going through each can help us think about ways to ensure all learners are engaged and supported through the unit. Above all, your lessons should be highly interactive and consistently require higher-level thinking. Worksheets should be kept to a minimum and should only be used when something more interactive and engaging just doesn't seem to work. As we go through the UDL Guidelines, I'll make suggestions for ways to integrate these into your cross-disciplinary lessons.

Guideline 1: Provide Options for Perception

- What auditory pieces do you plan on including in your unit?

- What short piece of literature, song, or poetry can you include for multiple readings and multiple types of viewing?

- What classroom supports will you put in place? Will you have a board dedicated to the unit? What information will you put up there? What student work will it include?

- What ways will students self-evaluate their progress? What will your culmination look like, and how will it ask students to present their knowledge in an engaging, reflective, and exciting way?

- Charting as you go is particularly relevant to this guideline. Giving students simultaneous auditory and visual stimulation is crucial for language learners and those with language-based learning differences, in addition to being valuable for all students to maximize their learning. These are particularly important in these units as students should be able to revisit the building block skills they need for the culmination at any time.

- Charts should be visually appealing and not just words. They should include symbols and imagery, as well as ample white space, so that students can engage in them in a multitude of ways without feeling overwhelmed.

- Music is a great way to integrate auditory processing. Doing a shared reading activity with a piece of music is a great way to discuss form, function, and process.

- When developing the jazz unit, I was thinking about many of my students with language-based learning differences—having an opportunity to simultaneously hear a song and read the lyrics provides the type of multisensory engagement they need. Shared reading is another great tool that provides multiple means of engagement, representation, and exposure.

Guideline 2: Provide Options for Language, Mathematical Expressions, and Symbols

- New words used through the unit should be put up in the classroom at the start of the unit or as they are introduced throughout the unit. Creating symbols to go with vocabulary words is a very useful tool to assist in comprehension.

- When you are planning your math integration activities, think about ways that you can remove the symbols from the problems you give. Mathematical reasoning problems don't tell students to follow a *given* pattern or rule; rather they ask them to use logic to plot their own path with the answer as the end. Building the process is the true apex. Giving words instead of symbols allows students to address what the problem is asking them and gives meaning to the symbols outside of the tricks and algorithms we teach that avoid critical reasoning. When your students are looking at multistep word problems, have them try to explain to someone else what they are supposed to find out. This way, they are processing the information in the problem before they begin working with any numbers or operations. Get them using their logical reasoning first; then they can use computation to follow the path they've charted.

Guideline 3: Provide Options for Comprehension

- Starting the unit by building background knowledge means that you'll want to start with a lot of your outside resources. Start with a read-aloud and, if you've found a relevant chapter book, use that as an anchor to return to throughout the unit and to introduce important material. Link lessons to what's going on in the book and provide opportunities to discuss the connections between the book and the unit.

- Having background information available to students at all times is critical. They should have a printout (or their own notes) that stay in their folders and can be used as a reference. Additionally, there should be a chart on the wall with relevant background information.

- Talking about the essential questions throughout the unit and posting them in the classroom allows students to continue to revisit them as they find them relevant.

Guideline 4: Provide Options for Physical Action

- Think about ways to get students moving. Centers are a great way to keep students moving every few minutes.

Doing brief activities where they get up and change partners is helpful. For journalism, we did mini interviews, where each student came up with their own question, and then they had 8 minutes in pairs to ask each other their questions and practice writing down the response; then they switched to a new partnership.

- Try to think about ways to keep them up and moving throughout a lesson. Developing a game for the unit that includes movement is a great way to get kids up and out of their seats. For a "said is dead" activity, I wrote on large charts, one in each corner of the room "replied," "yelled," "cried," and "whispered," and the kids then moved around to each chart, writing similar words that could be used.

- With this guideline, also think about allowing for flexible work environments. Some students might enjoy sitting outside or working on the floor for larger projects like drawing scale models. One of the nice parts about the independent work time students will have is that the classroom space can become more flexible and they can explore the ways they are most productive. If a student knows they work better sitting on the floor in a quiet corner than at their desk, they become a better advocate for themselves and are more aware that their focusing abilities vary based on the setting.

Guideline 5: Provide Options for Expression and Communication

- As with assessment, finding multiple modes for students to engage in a topic is crucial. In creating an outline, one student may draw pictures, while another may write in words, and another may record her voice explaining the plan.

- There should be a built-in flexibility within the lessons that allows students to process information in different ways, and in turn, communicate their learning in different ways.

Students who struggles with speaking may record their voice for the first presentation, and then for the next, may be challenged to say part of it out loud in the moment. Or, they may write out their speaking part and have it read out loud by the teacher.

- Always try to think about the ways that students feel most comfortable sharing their learning. Then find small and meaningful ways to stretch their edges and get them out of their comfort zone, without pushing beyond their capabilities.

Guideline 6: Provide Options for Executive Functions

- The key to this guideline is to build and support lower-level functioning (like organizing and planning) in order to allow higher-level tasks to be attainable (like following the directions of a multistep problem). Giving working memory a chance to both strengthen and disengage in the smaller tasks allows the more complex task to take center stage.

- Tracking sheets are a key component for supporting executive function. Students use these to manage their tasks in a thoughtful and scaffolded order, and to simultaneously see the larger task without being overwhelmed by it. A tracking sheet should organize the smaller tasks, allowing students to frequently move forward and feel successful, while also taking away the worry of "what do I do next?"

- Establishing a set organization for the unit helps make the process clear for students. They should know where they are going with their learning and what the expectations are for each activity. Create a dedicated space to store all work for each unit. A folder is a simple way to help students remain organized and remain responsible for keeping their work safe.

- Students who struggle with executive function may need additional pieces of support to guide them through cross-disciplinary units. I find checklists on the desk are a particularly useful tool. If a student forgets often to put papers away in the right place, a little note near the opening of the desk that says "Where should that piece of paper go?" can serve as a friendly reminder and doesn't require you to constantly revisit the student to ask the same question.

Guideline 7: Provide Options for Recruiting Interest

- This guideline is particularly relevant to crafting thematic units. These allow you to engage and utilize interest and intrigue as a tool to guide students into thinking about other disciplines in new ways.

- When crafting your lessons, think about students who are often disengaged: What are their interests? What makes the light in their eyes shine? Then try to think about how you can integrate something that they enjoy into the unit early on, giving them a topic and trajectory to hold on to and guide them through the unit. If a student loves sports, think about ways the ancient Greeks used sports, or how sports have helped immigrants assimilate into a new culture, or how sports writers develop their voice. Try to come up with a way for the student to find relevance in the theme, and design a lesson that gives them that as a starting point.

- If students are excited to begin a unit, they will carry that excitement through. A lot of this also comes from the teacher. If you are working on a topic you are genuinely excited about, this will model for them the type of joy that can come from learning more about new interests.

Guideline 8: Provide Options for Sustaining Effort and Persistence

- This guideline is particularly relevant to cross-disciplinary work as it relates to the unit's ability to challenge each student. Although there is a lot in this book about attending to those who learn best through less traditional ways, it is important to ensure that every student remains challenged and pushed to think further. There will be students in your class who immediately take to this work and may find the tasks easy. It's important that even your strongest students remain engaged and challenged.

- The culmination provides opportunities for sustaining effort and persistence as it allows for great differentiation of tasks. See "Planning to Create Options in Instruction," Chapter 5, for more on this.

Guideline 9: Provide Options for Self-Regulation

- This topic is largely covered when we go over assessment. One additional thing to keep in mind is that you will find that some students are so excited by the theme and the culmination that they want to do everything and anything. Helping them set boundaries and realistic goals will be crucial to their success. More isn't always better.

Appendix B

Universal Design for Learning Guidelines

The Universal Design for Learning Guidelines
Visit udlguidelines.cast.org for downloadable and printable copies.

CAST | Until learning has no limits

Provide multiple means of **Engagement**	Provide multiple means of **Representation**	Provide multiple means of **Action & Expression**
Affective Networks — The "WHY" of Learning	Recognition Networks — The "WHAT" of Learning	Strategic Networks — The "HOW" of Learning

Access

Provide options for
Recruiting Interest (7)
- Optimize individual choice and autonomy (7.1)
- Optimize relevance, value, and authenticity (7.2)
- Minimize threats and distractions (7.3)

Provide options for
Perception (1)
- Offer ways of customizing the display of information (1.1)
- Offer alternatives for auditory information (1.2)
- Offer alternatives for visual information (1.3)

Provide options for
Physical Action (4)
- Vary the methods for response and navigation (4.1)
- Optimize access to tools and assistive technologies (4.2)

Build

Provide options for
Sustaining Effort & Persistence (8)
- Heighten salience of goals and objectives (8.1)
- Vary demands and resources to optimize challenge (8.2)
- Foster collaboration and community (8.3)
- Increase mastery-oriented feedback (8.4)

Provide options for
Language & Symbols (2)
- Clarify vocabulary and symbols (2.1)
- Clarify syntax and structure (2.2)
- Support decoding of text, mathematical notation, and symbols (2.3)
- Promote understanding across languages (2.4)
- Illustrate through multiple media (2.5)

Provide options for
Expression & Communication (5)
- Use multiple media for communication (5.1)
- Use multiple tools for construction and composition (5.2)
- Build fluencies with graduated levels of support for practice and performance (5.3)

Internalize

Provide options for
Self Regulation (9)
- Promote expectations and beliefs that optimize motivation (9.1)
- Facilitate personal coping skills and strategies (9.2)
- Develop self-assessment and reflection (9.3)

Provide options for
Comprehension (3)
- Activate or supply background knowledge (3.1)
- Highlight patterns, critical features, big ideas, and relationships (3.2)
- Guide information processing and visualization (3.3)
- Maximize transfer and generalization (3.4)

Provide options for
Executive Functions (6)
- Guide appropriate goal-setting (6.1)
- Support planning and strategy development (6.2)
- Facilitate managing information and resources (6.3)
- Enhance capacity for monitoring progress (6.4)

Goal

Expert learners who are...

Purposeful & Motivated	Resourceful & Knowledgeable	Strategic & Goal-Directed

udlguidelines.cast.org | © CAST, Inc. 2018 | Suggested Citation: CAST (2018). Universal design for learning guidelines version 2.2 [graphic organizer]. Wakefield, MA: Author.

Acknowledgments

THERE ARE MANY PEOPLE WHO MADE THIS PROJECT POSSIBLE. First, this book would not have come together without the help of Billie Fitzpatrick. Her guidance and insight as an editor made going back through the book a joy. She gave me the tools I needed to sort through my overexplained ideas, giving me a pathway to clarity. Second, Sue Wiltz for believing in my voice as an educator and encouraging me to write this book. Third, David Gordon for seeing the value in teaching students in creative, exciting new ways and leading education into the future.

Additionally, I would not have known what education could look like without the guidance of many incredible educators. Carla Shalaby and Jeanette Epstein challenged me to see the power of education. Kathy Bacuyag Payson showed me what it is to know every student in your classroom, and Pat Katz taught me to believe in myself as an educator. Lisa Gilmore, one of the most amazing teachers to ever grace the classroom, opened my eyes to the power of creativity and joy.

Lastly, I want to acknowledge my lifelong editors: my first, my mom, Marsha, who has read everything I've written since I learned to write. Not only are her edits always a guiding light in my writing, but she taught me that growth and accomplishment come from rising to challenges. My dad, Jeffrey, for being there to talk through every idea and always believing in my insight. Finally, my husband, Caleb, my desk mate, thesaurus, misused comma finder, and my eternal cheerleader, whose belief in me makes me feel invincible. You make every endeavor, every challenge, everything, brighter.

About the Author

CHELSEA MIRO is a learning specialist (K–12) dedicated to creating individualized curricula for students with various learning needs and developing thematic, cross-disciplinary units for elementary and upper-level classrooms.

Chelsea received her bachelor's degree in American civilization and her master's degree in elementary education, both from Brown University, and has taught both third and fifth grades.

Chelsea is consistently working to improve the educational experiences of our youngest learners by exploring innovative approaches to teaching and learning.